ENDORSEMENTS FOR
Improvement Science in Education
A PRIMER

"This is an important book for educators who seek to use scientific means for solving all kinds of problems—particularly problems of educational equity. It addresses problems of practice, from instructional problems to organizational problems, and the nature of problems in general. As described by Hinnant-Crawford, improvement science will serve as a useful framework to undergird our continuous improvement efforts to alleviate inequities in education."

GLORIA LADSON-BILLINGS, PHD
PRESIDENT, NATIONAL ACADEMY OF EDUCATION
FELLOW, AMERICAN ACADEMY OF ARTS & SCIENCES
PROFESSOR EMERITA
UNIVERSITY OF WISCONSIN, MADISON

"Hinnant-Crawford has made clear the link between equity, justice, and improvement science. By focusing on the systems-level, improvement science empowers educational leaders to actively change the structures that perpetuate inequities for our children. This book offers a distinct set of tools for practitioners who strive to champion equity and justice as drivers of change."

JILL ALEXA PERRY, PHD
EXECUTIVE DIRECTOR,
CARNEGIE PROJECT ON THE EDUCATION DOCTORATE (CPED)
ASSOCIATE PROFESSOR OF THE PRACTICE
UNIVERSITY OF PITTSBURGH

"This book has arrived at exactly the right time for anyone who aspires to establish and nurture 'improvement science' as an essential foundation to better meet the needs of all students."

LYDIA DOBYNS
PRESIDENT AND CEO OF NEW TECH NETWORK

Improvement Science in Education

THE **IMPROVEMENT SCIENCE IN EDUCATION** SERIES

Improvement science originated in such fields as engineering and health care, but its principal foundation has been found to be an effective school improvement methodology in education. Although improvement science research is so quickly becoming a signature pedagogy and core subject area of inquiry in the field of educational leadership, the literature is still scant in its coverage of IS models. The Improvement Science in Education series is intended to be the most comprehensive collection of volumes to inform educators and researchers about problem analysis, utilization of research, development of solutions, and other practices can be employed to enhance and strengthen efforts at organizational improvement. This series concentrates on the elements faculty, students, and administrators need to enhance the reliability and validity of improvement or quality enhancement efforts.

BOOKS IN THE SERIES

The Educational Leader's Guide to Improvement Science:
Data, Design and Cases for Reflection
BY ROBERT CROW, BRANDI HINNANT-CRAWFORD, AND DEAN T. SPAULDING (2019)

The Improvement Science Dissertation in Practice:
A Guide for Faculty, Committee Members, and their Students
BY JILL ALEXA PERRY, DEBBY ZAMBO, AND ROBERT CROW (2020)

Improvement Science in Education: A Primer
BY BRANDI HINNANT-CRAWFORD (2020)

Teaching Improvement Science: A Pedagogical Guide
BY ROBERT CROW, BRANDI HINNANT-CRAWFORD, AND DEAN T. SPAULDING (2021)

Improvement Science: Methods for Researchers and Program Evaluators
BY ROBERT CROW, BRANDI HINNANT-CRAWFORD, AND DEAN T. SPAULDING (2021)

Improvement Together:
Case Studies of Networked Improvement Science Communities
BY ROBERT CROW, BRANDI HINNANT-CRAWFORD, AND DEAN T. SPAULDING (2021)

Improvement Science: In the Multidisciplinary Arena
BY ROBERT CROW, BRANDI HINNANT-CRAWFORD, AND DEAN T. SPAULDING (2022)

EDITORIAL SUBMISSIONS

Authors interested in having their manuscripts considered for publication in the Improvement Science in Education series are encouraged to send a prospectus, sample chapter, and CV to any one of the series editors:

Robert Crow (rcrow@email.wcu.edu)
Brandi Hinnant-Crawford (bnhinnantcrawford@wcu.edu)
Dean T. Spaulding (ds6494@yahoo.com)

Improvement Science in Education

A Primer

Brandi Nicole Hinnant-Crawford

Myers
Education
Press

Myers
Education
Press

Published by Myers Education Press, LLC
P.O. Box 424
Gorham, ME 04038

Myers Education Press is an academic publisher specializing in books, e-books, and digital content in the field of education. All of our books are subjected to a rigorous peer review process and produced in compliance with the standards of the Council on Library and Information Resources.

Library of Congress Cataloging-in-Publication Data available from Library of Congress.

13-digit ISBN 978-1-9755-0355-0 (paperback)
13-digit ISBN 978-1-9755-0354-3 (hard cover)
13-digit ISBN 978-1-9755-0356-7 (library networkable e-edition)
13-digit ISBN 978-1-9755-0357-4 (consumer e-edition)

Printed in the United States of America.

All first editions printed on acid-free paper that meets the American National Standards Institute Z39-48 standard.

Books published by Myers Education Press may be purchased at special quantity discount rates for groups, workshops, training organizations, and classroom usage. Please call our customer service department at 1-800-232-0223 for details.

Cover and text design by Sophie Appel

Visit us on the web at www.myersedpress.com to browse our complete list of titles.

For my heroines, women like Ella Baker and Septima Clark, immortalized in the history books, and those inscribed in my heart, namely, Evangeline Jones Artis Isler and Rose Artis Hinnant, the women who taught me ***by example*** to run on and see what the end is going to be. Who said, "If at first you don't succeed, try and try again," and told me never to *grow weary in well doing, for in due season we shall reap, if we faint not* (Galatians 6:9 KJV).

For Elizabeth Freedom and Elijah Justice, my twins. I pray you see in me a glimpse of the example of those who came before me.

For my doctoral students at Western Carolina University who have shown me the liberating power of improvement science in their organizations.

And for each of you, who I pray use improvement science as a tool for educational justice and to bring about equitable opportunities to learn for students from the cradle to beyond the doctorate. May our collective efforts transform the field to become the great equalizer instead of the great stratifier.

CONTENTS

SECTION ONE
Introduction—A Primer on Improvement Science

SECTION TWO
What Is the Exact Problem I'm Trying to Solve?

SECTION THREE
What Change Might I Introduce and Why?

Contents

LIST OF TABLES AND FIGURES

Tables

Figures

ACKNOWLEDGEMENTS

Writing a book is no small task, especially when it is your first single-authored text. There are so many individuals who deserve my gratitude. And I am sure in these acknowledgements I will unintentionally fail to capture someone.

I would like to begin with my friend, colleague, and mentor, Robert Crow, co-editor of this series on Improvement Science at Myers Education Press. I have to thank you for introducing me to the science of improvement and for teaching me about it. You also pointed me to the right places to continue to cultivate my knowledge about the science of improvement. If not for you, I would not be writing about this at all. So, thank you.

I also would like to thank Dean Spaulding, the other co-editor of this series. Your constant feedback and encouragement have been invaluable. Thank you for always responding to my random (and sometimes late night) texts. Your mentoring has meant more to me than you will ever know.

I would be remiss not to thank the giants on whose shoulders I stand. To those whose work and scholarship have cultivated my knowledge, I thank you. To the scholars of improvement science, thank you for advancing a methodology I wholeheartedly endorse. And to the scholars of equity in education, thank you for working for those in the margins and for providing me with examples throughout this text. And to the Black women in the academy who have created space for themselves and given me images to emulate —gratitude.

I also have to thank my colleagues and great friends who have been thought partners to help me think through different examples to ensure I had a broad range of representation from PK-12 and higher education. Thank you, Darrius Stanley and Emily Virtue, for letting me talk it out, for correcting my thought patterns, and for telling me things to consider. I cannot minimize the significance of your partnership. And to Jesse Whipple, my Six Sigma black belt friend, who read work on the methodologies new to me and let me know if I was going in the right direction—thank you. To copy editors and reviewers, iron sharpens iron, and your critique and direction has made my work stronger, and for that, you have my gratitude.

I would also like to thank my friends, colleagues, and mentors who encouraged me along the way. When I got discouraged and felt like I wanted to throw in the towel, you were the voices that drowned out my own. My mentor and big brother, Kofi Lomotey—thank you. To my sounding boards: Joscelyne Wilson, Crystal Sanders, Sheryl Croft, Dana Patterson, Tarnisha Casley, Tiffany Pogue, Charmion Rush, Terrence James, Breanna Delannoy, Ricardo Nazario y Colón, Jess Weiler, Heidi Von Dohlen, Erin Woodom-Coleman, my sorors, and all the clergy in my corner—your words, your push, your "keep going" are why this happened.

To my sister, Brianna Hinnant, who always seems so proud of me—and is my social media hype man. I love you. I know your influence on our field is just beginning.

To my father, Johnny Wooten, who has always seen more potential in me than I saw in myself—for your encouragement I am forever grateful.

To my mother, Rose Artis Hinnant, sincere gratitude. Thank you for taking my children and giving me space to write. I would take off in the morning and come back in the evening, and I knew while I was gone they were in perfect hands. Your encouragement and support were tangible—and your inspiration is why you have two daughters following in your footsteps.

Elizabeth and Elijah, to whom I feel like I constantly have to apologize for being preoccupied with work. As I said in my dissertation, and it remains true today, Mommy wants other children to have the same opportunities that she will ensure that you have. Therefore, it is incumbent upon me to do this work. I appreciate the grace you give me, as a single career-mom who cannot be in all places at all times. I love you.

And to the God of my salvation—it is my prayer that improvement science can become a tool of liberation that will serve *the least of these*. I hope this work is pleasing in Your sight.

SECTION ONE

Introduction—A Primer on Improvement Science

Improvement science is a methodological framework that is undergirded by foundational principles that guide *scholar-practitioners* to define problems, understand how the system produces the problems, identify changes to rectify the problems, test the efficacy of those changes, and spread the changes (if the change is indeed an improvement). [That's a mouthful! Read it again if you have to!] Improvement science is a systematic approach to continuous improvement in complex organizations, guided by three foundational questions:

1. What is the exact problem I am trying to solve? or What am I trying to accomplish?
2. What change might I introduce to solve it (and why)?
3. How will I know that change is an improvement?

The purpose of this primer on improvement science is twofold: to introduce or expand your knowledge of improvement science and to illustrate its capacity to be used as a methodological tool for equity and educational justice. Each chapter is written to illuminate the science as a framework for inquiry as well as describe its applicability to complex problems of practice, particularly those that address the needs of traditionally marginalized students. In this introduction, I will share my assumptions about you (the reader), my unconventional approach to writing, and an overview of how the text is organized.

If you have picked up this primer, you are probably a scholar-practitioner (or one in the making); this means you have dual identities. You are rooted in practice, but you want practice to be informed by who you are as a scholar. And if you are a practitioner, realistically, you probably do not have time to read the latest journal articles on every problem you are facing. While most scholars can pick a single topic to fixate on their whole career, practitioners are dealing with a myriad of issues at any one time. For example, Albert Bandura has built a career developing social cognitive theory. As a school counselor, you may have some interest in different types of self-efficacy, but you are also interested in trauma-informed practices, wrap around services for students, bullying in the classroom, and a host of other issues. Bandura's work can inform yours, but you will not be conducting studies to understand self-efficacy to the extent he has. However, you may try a program with some students to see if their academic sense of self-efficacy increases as a result of it. You may use instruments Bandura or his students created to measure growth in self-efficacy. But you are most interested in how his work can inform your practice, not how you can conduct research to inform his theory.

I make several assumptions about who you are in the way this text is written. I assume you are a practitioner and I assume you are from the field of education. I also make another assumption that I must be explicit about; I assume you want to improve education because you care about students (be they in pre-school or graduate school). I assume disparities in access to educational opportunities unnerve you, and you are looking for a systematic way to tackle education's big problems like equity and injustice. Therefore, my examples will be rooted in educational organizations and will be centered around issues of justice, equity, and inclusivity. Throughout this text, I will ask you to keep in mind two parties who are necessary for improving for equity: *who is involved* with the improvement process and *who will be impacted.* Can you use improvement science to make a process more efficient while maintaining the status quo? Absolutely! But that is not how I hope you will use it.

In this text, I use the second person pronoun, "you," throughout. I want you to see yourself as the change agent in your organization. It may be an unconventional form of writing, but it is intentional. I want you to see yourself as the scholar-practitioner. As Ella Baker encouraged youth to be the catalyst for change, I want to encourage you to be the champion for improvement and equitable outcomes in your organization.

The layout of this text is quite straightforward. This primer is divided into three sections:

- I. A Primer on Improvement Sciencee
- II. What is the exact problem I am trying to solve? What am I trying to accomplish?
- III. What change might I introduce and why? How will I know the change is an improvement?

Part I pushes you to acknowledge the science in improvement science. After a brief description of the relationship between research and education and an examination of the philosophical underpinnings of improvement science in Part I, this text is organized around the six principles of improvement science espoused in Bryk, Gomez, Grunow, and LeMahieu's (2015) text, *Learning to Improve: How America's Schools Can Get Better at Getting Better,* and what I refer to as the essential improvement science questions. While I discuss the principles in the order they are introduced in Bryk's text, I do not want to give the illusion that these principles are steps in a process. Continuous improvement is a cyclical process, and improvement science is one of many frameworks to guide continuous improvement. As illustrated below, in figure I.1, the improvement science essential questions map on to the generic steps of continuous improvement.

Figure I.1. Crosswalk Between Continuous Improvement Steps and Improvement Science Essential Questions

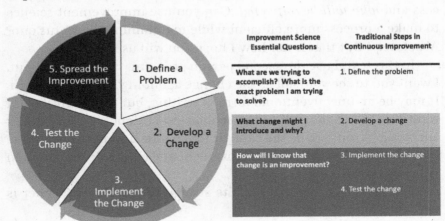

	Improvement Science Essential Questions	Traditional Steps in Continuous Improvement
	What are we trying to accomplish? What is the exact problem I am trying to solve?	1. Define the problem
	What change might I introduce and why?	2. Develop a change
	How will I know that change is an improvement?	3. Implement the change
		4. Test the change

While the questions map on nicely, the principles do not. Conversely, the principles are guidance for improvement praxis and can be revisited during any portion of the improvement journey. For example, you need to be able to *see the system* (principle 3) to successfully define the problem, develop a change, implement a change, test the change, and spread improvement. The difference in language, in the continuous improvement steps, is intentional; change is used in steps two through four, and improvement is used in step five. Only after the impact of a change has been assessed can that change be deemed an improvement. You only want to spread improvement.

The portion of the book examining the improvement science principles is divided into two parts because in general, you have to define and understand the problem before you can develop initiatives to improve it. Chapters on principles, chapters three through nine, define what each principle means and describe tools you can use while employing that principle. Every chapter also includes examples from K-12, community college, or university contexts and questions to prompt reflection during your improvement journey to ensure you are improving with equity in mind. I conclude this text with a personal endorsement of the methodology, explaining how my positionality and axiology lead me to write this text.

As a primer, this text is admittedly not as comprehensive as some others, such as the 500-plus page *The Improvement Guide: A Practical Approach to Enhancing Organizational Performance.* When I introduce a text with a book icon like that pictured below, serious students will take note and consider adding that book to their libraries.

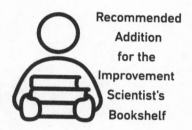

Recommended Addition for the Improvement Scientist's Bookshelf

The first two you need are *The Improvement Guide* (Langley, Moen, Nolan, Nolan, Norman & Provost, 2009) and *Learning to Improve* (Bryk, Gomez, Grunow & LeMahieu, 2015). For improvement scientists in education, these texts are must reads!

In 1964, educator and activist Septima P. Clark (1898–1987) challenged those who care about freedom to be "action-research minded. We have to take a look at where we are and where we want to be" (Clark, 1964, p. 117). While this text explores improvement science and not action research, the premise is still the same. We have to unearth our problems, understand our current systems, and have prophetic imagination about what can be, and then work to bring that about. Improvement science is a methodology that can help us do just that.

Clark, S. (1964). Literacy and liberation. *Freedomways, 4*(1), 113–124.

Bryk, A. S., Gomez, L. M., Grunow, A., & LeMahieu, P. G. (2015). *Learning to improve: How America's schools can get better at getting better.* Cambridge, MA: Harvard Education Press.

Langley, G. J., Moen, R. D., Nolan, K. M., Nolan, T. W., Norman, C. L., & Provost, L. P. (2009). *The improvement guide: A practical approach to enhancing organizational performance.* Charlottesville, VA: Wiley.

CHAPTER ONE

Research, Science, and Education

This initial chapter of *Improvement Science in Education: A Primer*, on research, science, and education, is designed specifically for the practitioner. It explores the historical relationship between education and scientific study. This section serves as a foundation to help illustrate how improvement science is informed by, yet distinct from, other types of research in education. If you have not had an educational or social science research methods course recently, this section was designed with you in mind.

The Evolution of Science

It is difficult to pinpoint the origins of science. The nature of human curiosity has always led people to observe the world around them. Medicine men and women, sky gazers, agriculturalists, and more have manipulated elements to change outcomes for as long as humans have inhabited the earth. Wisdom in proverbs and maxims throughout ancient and modern times was probably based on tried and tested theories.

7

Ibn al-Haytham (965–1040), Islamic scientist born in what would become modern-day Iraq, is often credited with being one of the first empiricists. Alias and Hanapi (2016) explain that Islam identifies five sources of revelation, two of which are the senses and intellect, and those were the basics of al-Haytham's epistemology. While he explicitly studied optics and light, al-Haytham explained:

> Truths are obscure, the ends hidden, the doubts manifold, the minds turbid, the reasonings various; the premises are gleaned from the senses and the senses (which are our tools) are not immune from error. (as cited in Alias and Hanapi, 2016, p. 90)

Al-Haytham is credited with designing a four-step process: observe, hypothesize, experiment, and conclude. Galileo (1564–1642) and Francis Bacon (1561–1626) follow al-Haytham with significant contributions to our understandings of modern (Western) science. Similar to al-Haytham, Bacon suggests an inductive reasoning process that proceeds from "observations to axiom to law" (Moen & Norman, 2006, p. 3).

At this point in reading, you may be questioning—what does this have to do with improvement science? Why do the origins matter? When you examine the lives of ancient scientists you find, like improvement scientists, they were not discipline-specific. They had a method for understanding the world and attempting to modify it, and that is what improvement science is. While this text focuses on applications to education, this science is not content-specific like biology or chemistry, but advancing improvement science in education pulls wisdom about the nature of improvement from business, engineering, and medicine—and from intellectual traditions all over the world.

Science and Education

Science and education are often put together when considering the curricular content in the natural sciences. But this text is not about science education. Instead, I hope you are interested in the science behind education. Suter explains, "Educational researchers are committed to improving the quality of education by increasing their knowledge" about both the art of teaching and the science of learning (Suter, 2012, p. 4). Inherent in educational research is the goal of educational improvement. Educational researcher and methodologist Slavin argues in his (2002) distinguished lecture on educational research that the scientific revolution that "utterly transformed medicine, agriculture, transportation, technology, [etc.]...almost completely bypassed education" (Slavin, 2002, p. 16). He goes on to say that if Rip Van Winkle had been a medical doctor or engineer, he would have awoken to find himself unemployed, but that if he had been a teacher, he could probably have picked up where he left off. So, where are the breakthroughs in the science of education?

Despite Slavin's critique, the field of education has been heavily influenced by research. The enterprise of public education is nearly 200 years old in the United States, and the enterprise of educational research is 103 years old, if measured by proxy of the age of the American Educational Research Association. Both of these communities, which fail to communicate as often as necessary, were heavily influenced by scientific management, or Taylorism. Taylor's *Principals of Scientific Management* (1911) articulated that the role of experts (educational scholars) was to identify the single best way to achieve a task through the use of "time and motion" studies (Murnane and Willett, 2010, p. 4). This epistemology was translated into educational research. Murnane and Willett (2010) explicate:

> Although Taylor was careful not to apply his methods to any process as complicated as education, many educational researchers were less cautious...[Frank] Spaulding described three essentials for applying scientific management to education. He stipulated that we must: (a) measure results, (b) compare the conditions and methods under which results are secured, and (c) adopt consistently the conditions and methods that produce the best results. (p. 4)

Complicated is the word Murnane and Willett (2010) use to describe education. Throughout this text, I will describe the nature of education as complex. While this approach may indeed work in a factory where the input is static; in educational systems, the inputs are students, each complete with their own life and history and decision-making capacity and agency. It is, to be overly simplistic, quite different.

Taylorism simultaneously influenced the goals of educational research and the management of schools. In the latter half of the 20th century, there was a movement to centralize control of schools. This reengineering of the educational structure, from local to a more centralized, managerial structure was a direct derivative of scientific management. The goal was to run schools like factories, "like the manager of a cotton mill, the superintendent of schools could supervise employees, keep the entire enterprise technically up to date, and monitor the uniformity and quality of the product," in this case, education (Tyack, 1974, p. 40). In both educational research and educational practice, the goal became to identify the single best way to educate and then to standardize that process across different contexts. As such, the Tayloristic approach disregarded the agency of the teachers and the heterogeneity of the students and their contexts.

The truth is, educators and educational researchers are still searching for the one best way to educate. And the field has recognized that research plays a role in determining what is "best practice." Yet, as the discourse has changed from "best practice" to "evidence-based practice" and from "effective schools" to "comprehensive school reform," our outcomes are not substantially different.

A Turning Point

The same year Slavin (2002) delivered his keynote, questioning the impact and contributions of educational research and the rigor behind the enterprise, the What Works Clearinghouse (WWC) was created. The purpose of the WWC was to "evaluate and synthesize research evidence for the effectiveness of educational interventions and to serve as a central and trusted source of scientific evidence for what works in education" (Song & Herman, 2010, p. 251). The creation of the WWC was in direct response to the passing of No Child Left Behind legislation (in 2001), which referenced evidence-based or research-based practice 110 times throughout the legislation. Also, during 2002, the National Research Council of the National Academy of Sciences issued a report with three premises for educational research: 1) true experiments were necessary to make causal claims, 2) qualitative research was necessary and useful, and 3) education can be transformed by research just like other fields (Gersten & Hitchcock, 2011).

The report heralded the need for randomized controlled trials (RCTs) or true experiments to establish casual relationships between interventions and outcomes. A *true experiment* is a study where individuals are randomly assigned (meaning everyone has an equal chance of being assigned) to treatment and control groups. Often after an initial pretest or establishing of the baseline of each group, the treatment group is given the intervention while the control group is not. Subsequently, members of each group are measured on some outcome after the treatment is administered. There are a number of true experiments in education, such as the Tennessee Star study about class size or the evaluation studies of Success for All reading intervention. Experiments are often hard to implement in education, but proponents of RCTs explain they are difficult to implement in other fields as well, and that is not an excuse for educational researchers.

If you are a student affairs professional at a state university or an instructional coach at an elementary school, you may have little interest in knowing the ins and outs of educational research history or the preferred methods. But you may be curious as to why, after at least 100 years of educational research, we have not had dramatic improvements in the field of education. While there is a well-known gap between research and practice, the roots of the problem may be a little deeper than that. Speaking to medical professionals about improvement in the *Journal of the American Medical Association*, Berwick explained:

> To improve care, evaluation should retain and share information on both mechanisms (i.e., the ways in which specific social programs actually produce social changes) and contexts (i.e., local conditions that could have influenced the outcomes of interest).

Evaluators and medical journals will have to recognize that, by
itself, the usual OXO[1] experimental paradigm is not up to this task.
It is possible to rely on other methods without sacrificing rigor.
Many assessment techniques developed in engineering and used in
quality improvement—statistical process control, time series analysis, simulations, and factorial experiments—have more power to
inform about mechanisms and contexts than do RCTs, as do ethnography, anthropology, and other qualitative methods. (Berwick,
2008, p. 1183)

Research is evaluated in terms of its validity. In short, *validity*
means accuracy. Experimental research (and quantitative research
in general) deals with two types of validity: internal validity and external validity. An experiment has *internal validity* when no other variable besides the treatment can be argued to influence the outcome.
Only when this is the case can you make causal claims. *External
validity* deals with generalizability. *Generalizability* is the extent
to which the findings of the experiment in question can generalize
to another setting. Usually, there is a tradeoff. As internal validity
increases, external validity decreases. As Berwick talks about under-
stating mechanisms and contexts, he is discussing other variables
(such as the context) that may influence the outcomes. Experiments
often tell us *if* an intervention can work, whereas improvement science tells us *how, under what conditions, and for whom* an intervention works. To be explicit, I am not elevating one over the other.
Both are necessary.

Types of Educational Research

If you are working on your EdD in curriculum and instruction, or
your PhD in education policy, you can skim this section (you know,
the graduate student skim). Throughout this text, I compare and

---

1   In describing research designs, "O" signifies measurement or obser-
    vation and "X" signifies treatment or intervention. An OXO design is a
    pretest-posttest research design.

contrast improvement science to other types of educational research, so you can understand what it is, and what it is not. This section will give you a brief, high-level overview of other types of educational research as a foundation for understanding improvement science.

John Creswell, well-known research methodologist, argues that researchers from every paradigm are guided by some philosophy. Improvement scientists are no different. Creswell explains:

> Philosophically, researchers make claims about what is knowledge (ontology), how we know it (epistemology), what values go into it (axiology), how we write about it (rhetoric), and the processes for studying it (methodology). (Creswell, 2003, p. 6)

W.E. Deming (1994), the father of quality improvement, is perhaps the grandfather of improvement science. His ontological definition of knowledge articulates:

> A statement, if it conveys knowledge, predicts future outcome, with risk of being wrong, and that it fits without failure observations of the past. Rational prediction requires theory and builds knowledge through systematic revision and extension of theory based on comparison of prediction with observation. (Deming, 1994, p. 102)

Positivism, Post-positivism, and Quantitative Research

In this sense, improvement science may seem positivistic or post-positivistic in orientation, since it is seeking to understand cause-and-effect relationships. *Positivism and post-positivism* are a research framework associated with traditional scientific study. Do you remember the scientific method in third grade? When you formed your hypothesis and then conducted your experiment? This approach is positivistic in nature; it is deterministic and wants to explain, predict, and determine cause-and-effect relationships. Positivism asserts that truth exists; post-positivists agree truth exists, but argue that we can never be certain or "positive" that we know what it is.

Research in the positivistic paradigm is often quantitative, and answers questions like:

- If I add a new orientation for my online transfer students, will they be more likely to complete their first semester?
- If I increase reading instruction by 10 minutes daily, will my students perform better on the end-of-year exam?

The cause and effect questions are positivistic and quantitative. *Quantitative research* seeks to uncover general truths that can explain phenomena in most circumstances; in that sense, it is reductionist. Parsimony, where a phenomenon is explained with the fewest variables possible, is a priority. The goal of quantitative research is to be generalizable. Quantitative research seeks to predict and explain, and tries to model truth with numbers. There are a number of types of quantitative research designs: experiments, quasi-experiments, causal comparative studies, correlational studies, single-subject, time-series, and more. For an in-depth examination of different types of quantitative research designs, see (Creswell & Guetterman, 2019; Krathwohl, 2009; Murnane & Willett, 2010; Schneider, Carnoy, Kilpatrick, Schmidt & Shavelson, 2007). To distinguish quantitative research from qualitative, examine the root of the word: QUANTitative. Think QUANTitative and QUANTity (numerical data).

In Deming's statement of what is knowledge, his articulation sets the expectation of a deductive approach to acquiring knowledge. *Deductive reasoning* begins with an answer, a theory, or hypothesis about what is happening, and then uses observations (data) to confirm or verify the initial premise is correct. Deming begins with theory, moves on to data, then to confirms or revises the theory.

Constructivism and Qualitative Research

Another common research paradigm is *constructivism*. In contrast to post-positivist, constructivists believe that truth is constructed, and to some extent is "in the eye of the beholder." Instead of being reductionist, constructivism leads "the researcher to look for the complexity of views rather than narrowing meaning into a few categories or ideas" (Creswell, 2003, p. 8). In constructivist research, there is somewhat of a shift in power; the participants are the experts on the phenomena in question, and only through collection and synthesis of their voices does the researcher arrive at some understanding of what is under study. You will see elements of constructivism in defining the problem in improvement science.

Constructivism is often associated with qualitative research. The purpose of qualitative research is to develop theory and provide thick, rich descriptions of a phenomenon in a particular instance. Quantitative research is associated with breadth (generalizability); *qualitative research* is associated with depth of understanding. The goal of qualitative research is not generalizability, as it is with quantitative research. Instead, the goal is accurate descriptions and interpretations of the specific case under study. Maxwell (1992) refers to this as descriptive and interpretive validity. There are a several types of qualitative research designs, including but not limited to: phenomenology (Moran, 2002), grounded theory (Strauss & Corbin, 1997), narrative inquiry (Connelly & Clandinin, 1990), ethnography (Hammersley & Atkinson, 2007), discourse analysis (Weiss & Wodack, 2007), case study (Merriam, 1988; Yin, 2017), and biography (Creswell & Poth, 2016). For more details on qualitative research designs, see the works of qualitative methodologists (Creswell & Poth, 2016; Miles, Huberman, Saldaña, & Maxwell, 2005; Patton, 2002). Qualitative research and constructivism take an inductive approach to understanding phenomena. *Inductive reasoning* begins with the data (the voices or observations), develops patterns, and then specifies a theory.

Pragmatism and Improvement Science

Pragmatism is an additional research paradigm, and the one most closely associated with improvement science. Unlike post-positivism which wants to test theories (quantitative research), and constructivism which wants to develop theories (qualitative research), *pragmatism* is a research paradigm primarily concerned with "what works." Biesenthal explains that pragmatism "aims to uncover practical knowledge—knowledge that works in a particular situation. The acquired knowledge is evaluated by reference to its problem-solving capacity in everyday life rather than its universal applicability, which makes pragmatism a fruitful tool for action researchers" (2014, p. 648). In many ways, pragmatic researchers seem to be well aligned with the scholar-practitioner, who is primarily concerned about uncovering new ways to do their job better. Pragmatists do not subscribe to a particular research domain, such as quantitative or qualitative. On the contrary, "instead of methods being important, the problem is most important, and researchers use all approaches to understand the problem" (Creswell, 2003, p. 11).

Theory-based vs. Problem-based

Some educational methodologists explain that research in education can be crudely divided into two categories, theory-based and problem-based (Suter, 2011). Theory-based research is more traditional in nature, and is designed to answer some questions extant in scholarly literature (such as in positivist or constructivist paradigms). Problem-based research is used to address problems that occur in the field. Pragmatic research designs are most apt to tackle problem-based research. Action research (McIntyre, 2008) and program evaluation (Spaulding, 2013) are probably the most notable forms of problem-based research.

The Critical, Participatory, Advocacy, and Emancipatory Paradigm

One final research paradigm that goes by a number of names is the *critical, participatory, advocacy, and emancipatory paradigm.* While some research paradigms strive to illustrate their objectivity, researchers involved in critical approaches are explicit about their intent for social transformation. Their axiology is more explicit than some of the other forms. These researchers are intentional about doing research "with" and not "on" marginalized communities, and moving from findings to action (like pragmatist). While constructivists elevate the voice of the participants, those from the critical, participatory, advocacy, and emancipatory paradigm argue that constructivists do not go far enough in their attempts to bring about change. Researchers from this broad and varied paradigm are often guided by critical theory (Leonardo, 2004), critical race theory (Tate, 1997), feminist theory, and/or queer theory (Dilley, 1999; Stein & Plummer, 1994). This paradigm's approach to research is commonly qualitative. Hood (2001), who examines the contributions of early African American evaluation researchers, said one of the common characteristics of their culturally responsive approach to evaluation was including qualitative research. Hood (2001) explains:

> That a rich description of the program and the context in which it functioned were critical to achieving something more than a superficial understanding of the program. The message seemed clear that qualitative data—observations, interviews, document reviews—could and should have equal importance as quantitative data in the evaluation of a program. (p. 35)

The value of the voice is elevated in this paradigm. Although typically, research in this paradigm is qualitative, methodological scholars have shown us that the critical nature is not reserved for one type of data. Critical multicultural scholar, Christine Sleeter, details the potential for quantitative liberatory research and gives insights on why it is not commonly found:

> It is quite possible that debates about the limitations of positivism have produced generations of scholars who have not learned to use the tools of positivist research such as gathering quantitative data, having learned to equate such tools with how they have been used historically. Quantitative research can be used for liberatory as well as oppressive ends. Scholars such as Carter G. Woodson and W. E. B. DuBois embraced the empirical paradigm because they viewed it as a way in which to gather "objective" data that would undercut widespread misconceptions about African Americans . . . Positivist or postpositivist emancipatory research that connects generalizations with local contexts and viewpoints can offer useful support for policy change and program development. (Sleeter, 2000, p. 25)

Improvement science has aspects of positivism and constructivism, and is undergirded by pragmatism; but if directed toward issues of equity and justice, it, too, can be a critical and participatory tool for liberation. In this primer, I will introduce you to the basics of improvement science and promote its liberatory potential. If you choose to use it to increase your efficiency while maintaining the status quo, that is your choice. However, if you are seeking a methodological tool to help you engineer a more just society by improving schools, colleges, and universities, improvement science may be the tool for you.

With the diversity of educational research and most of it being aimed at improving educational organization or approaches to teaching and learning, you may wonder why improvement science is even necessary in the field of education. Or you may be thinking—if it has elements of positivism, constructivism, pragmatism, and liberatory paradigms, is it simply more of the same? Chapter 2, "What is Improvement Science? Why Do You Need It," answers these questions by articulating the need for improvement science and its distinction from traditional forms of education research.

Key Terms

- **Constructivism**—Constructivism, often associated with qualitative research, is a research paradigm that asserts truth is constructed, and that truth varies depending on perspective.
- **Critical, participatory, advocacy, and emancipatory Research**—Critical, participatory, advocacy, and emancipatory research paradigms are concerned with social change. The objective of this research is to elevate the voice of marginalized, and to do research *with* and not *on* marginalized populations.
- **Deductive reasoning**—Deductive reasoning begins with theory and moves from theory, to data, to confirmation or revision of the theory.
- **External validity**—External validity is often referred to as generalizability. External validity answers the question: *Are the study's findings true (accurate) for those outside of the study?*
- **Generalizability**—Generalizability asks to what extent a study's findings generalize to other contexts. It is also known as external validity.

- **Inductive reasoning**—Inductive reasoning begins with data or observations, and moves from data, to patterns, to theory.
- **Internal validity**—Interval validity deals with the question: *Are the findings true (or accurate) for the participants in the study?* In quantitative research, where there is a treatment administered or a particular covariate in question, validity is determined when no other factor can be argued to influence the outcome besides the variable in question.
- **Positivism/post-positivism**—Positivism is an approach to research (research paradigm) that asserts a truth does exist. Positivism is predecessor of post-positivism, which also believes truth exists, but researchers can never be certain that they have reached the truth.
- **Pragmatism**—Pragmatism is a research paradigm concerned with how research and its findings can be applied to improve practical functions. Essentially, pragmatists seek to answer the question: *What works?*
- **Qualitative research**—Qualitative research is an approach designed to generate theory by exploring a phenomenon in detail and providing thick, rich descriptions. The goal is depth not breadth.
- **Quantitative research**—Quantitative research generally tests theories. Quantitative research seeks to uncover general truths that can explain phenome in most circumstances. There is a premium on parsimony, explaining a phenomenon with as few variables as possible. The goal of quantitative research, in most cases, is to produce results that are generalizable.
- **True experiment**—A true experiment is a study that compares the outcomes of two groups: a treatment group and a control group. These two groups are assigned using random assignment, meaning everyone in the sample has an equal chance of being assigned to either group. The treatment group experiences some treatment or intervention where the control group does not. The outcomes of the two groups are compared. True experiments, or randomized controlled trials, are considered the gold standard in research. Quasi-experiments are a similar type of research design, but lack the random assignment.

- **Validity**—Validity means accuracy. Conceptually, it deals with the question of whether findings from a particular study can be trusted. Quantitative research deals with two types of validity internal validity and external validity. Qualitative research uses different criteria for evaluation, and is assessed by its descriptive validity, interpretive validity, and trustworthiness.

References

Alias, M. S., & Hanapi, M. S. (2016). The Epistemological Aspect of Ibn Al-Haytham's Scientific Thought. *Sains Humanika, 8*(3-2).

Berwick, D. M. (2008). The science of improvement. *JAMA, 299*(10), 1182–1184.

Biesenthal, C. (2014). Pragmatism. In D. Coghlan & M. Brydon-Miller (Eds.), *The Sage Encyclopedia of Action Research* (Vol. 1-2, pp. 648–650). London: Sage.

Connelly, F. M., & Clandinin, D. J. (1990). Stories of experience and narrative inquiry. *Educational Researcher, 19*(5), 2–14.

Corbin, J., & Strauss, A. (2008). *Basics of qualitative research* (3rd ed.). Thousand Oaks, CA: Sage publications.

Creswell, J. W. (2003). *Research design: Qualitative, quantitative, and mixed method approaches* (2nd ed.). Thousand Oaks, CA: Sage.

Creswell, J. W., & Guetterman, T. C. (2019). *Educational research: Planning, conducting, and evaluating quantitative and qualitative research*. Upper Saddle River, NJ: Pearson.

Creswell, J. W., & Poth, C. N. (2016). *Qualitative inquiry and research design: Choosing among five approaches* (4th ed.). Thousand Oaks, CA: Sage.

Deming, W. E. (2000/1994). *The new economics for industry, government, education*. Cambridge, MA: MIT Press.

Dilley, P. (1999). Queer theory: Under construction. *International Journal of Qualitative Studies in Education, 12*(5), 457–472.

Gersten, R., & Hitchcock, J. (2009). What is credible evidence in education? The role of the What Works Clearinghouse in informing the process. In S.I. Donaldson, C.A. Christie, & M. M. Mark (Eds.), *What counts as credible evidence in applied research and evaluation practice?* (pp. 78–95). Thousand Oaks, CA: Sage.

Hammersley, M., & Atkinson, P. (2007). *Ethnography: Principles in practice*. Philadelphia, PA: Routledge.

Hood, S. (2001). Nobody knows my name: In praise of African American evaluators who were responsive. *New Directions for Evaluation, 2001*(92), 31–44.

Krathwohl, D. R. (2009). *Methods of educational and social science research: The logic of methods*. Long Grove, IL: Waveland Press.

Leonardo, Z. (2004). Critical social theory and transformative knowledge: The functions of criticism in quality education. *Educational Researcher, 33*(6), 11–18.

Maxwell, J. A. (2005). *Qualitative research design: An interactive approach* (2nd ed.). Thousand Oaks, CA: Sage publications.

McIntyre, A. (2008). *Participatory action research*. Thousand Oaks, CA: Sage publications.

Merriam, S. B. (1988). *Case study research in education: A qualitative approach*. San Francisco, CA: Jossey-Bass.

Miles, M. B., Huberman, A. M., & Saldaña, J. (2014). *Qualitative data analysis: A methods sourcebook* (3rd ed.). Thousand Oaks, CA: Sage.

Moen, R., & Norman, C., Evolution of the PDCA Cycle. http://pkpinc.com/files/NA01MoenNormanFullpaper.pdf. Accessed June 7, 2012.

Moran, D. (2002). *Introduction to phenomenology*. Philadelphia, PA: Routledge.

Murnane, R. J., & Willett, J. B. (2010). *Methods matter: Improving causal inference in educational and social science research*. Oxford, UK: Oxford University Press.

Patton, M. Q. (2002). *Qualitative evaluation and research methods* (3rd ed.). Thousand Oaks, CA: Sage.

Schneider, B., Carnoy, M., Kilpatrick, J., Schmidt, W. H., & Shavelson, R. J. (2007). *Estimating causal effects using experimental and observational design*. Washington, DC: American Educational & Research Association.

Slavin, R. E. (2002). Evidence-based education policies: Transforming educational practice and research. *Educational Researcher, 31*(7), 15–21.

Sleeter, C. E. (2000). Chapter 6: Epistemological diversity in research on pre-service teacher preparation for historically underserved children. *Review of Research in Education, 25*(1), 209–250.

Song, M., & Herman, R. (2010). Critical issues and common pitfalls in designing and conducting impact studies in education: Lessons learned from the What Works Clearinghouse (Phase I). *Educational Evaluation and Policy Analysis, 32*(3), 351–371.

Spaulding, D. T. (2013). *Program evaluation in practice: Core concepts and examples for discussion and analysis.* Hoboken, NJ: John Wiley & Sons.

Stein, A., & Plummer, K. (1994). "I can't even think straight": "Queer" theory and the missing sexual revolution in sociology. *Sociological Theory, 12*(2), 178–187.

Strauss, A., & Corbin, J. M. (1997). *Grounded theory in practice.* Thousand Oaks, CA: Sage.

Suter, W. N. (2011). *Introduction to educational research: A critical thinking approach.* Thousand Oaks, CA: Sage.

Tate, W. F., IV. (1997). Chapter 4: Critical race theory and education: History, theory, and implications. *Review of Research in Education, 22*(1), 195–247.

Tyack, D. B. (1974). *The one best system: A history of American urban education* (Vol. 95). Cambridge, MA: Harvard University Press.

Weiss, G., & Wodak, R. (Eds.). (2007). *Critical discourse analysis.* New York, NY: Palgrave Macmillan.

Yin, R. K. (2017). *Case study research and applications: Design and methods.* Thousand Oaks, CA: Sage.

CHAPTER TWO

What is Improvement Science? Why Do You Need It?

The Need for Improvement Science

After reading chapter 1, and learning the general goal of educational research is to improve education, you may be asking, why do we need improvement science? Improvement science is a methodic way of improving; it is distinct from evaluation or impact studies. Those studies, often employing sophisticated statistical analyses such as hierarchical linear modeling, regression discontinuity, or propensity score matching, estimate the effect of some improvement, but they do not guide you through the process of improving. This is what makes improvement science distinct from educational research. In this chapter, I will attempt to persuade you to believe it is necessary to add improvement science into your arsenal of techniques for improving education; I will explore the varying definitions of improvement science put forth by scholars, and I will elucidate the theoretical underpinnings of improvement science.

After centuries of educational research, why do we need improvement science? The simple answer is that educational research alone has not yielded the results we need. According to the Condition of

Education 2019, published by the National Center for Educational Statistics, only 37% of 12th-graders were at or above proficient in reading and only 25% of 12th-graders were proficient in mathematics on the National Assessment of Educational Progress (NAEP) in 2015. Similarly, in higher education, the graduation rate for 150% of time to degree in two-year colleges (which essentially means three years for those enrolled in a two-year degree program) was 30.3%. While the six-year graduation rate at four-year universities was higher, at 59.7%, this is still much lower than what educators in higher education would like to see. Despite our research on literacy, numeracy, retention, and persistence, our outcomes are not what we desire. And if these outcomes were disaggregated in order to view traditionally underserved communities, we would find even more alarming outcomes. While research has increased what we know about education, it has not drastically changed the way we do business. Put another way, within the articulation of need for improvement science is:

> A diagnosis of why the last century of education R&D [research and development] has not brought the same advances found in other fields like medicine, agriculture, manufacturing, or technology. The R&D capacity in education is not well suited to addressing current challenges: it is underfunded, values theory development over practical solutions, fails to transform the wisdom of practice into a professional knowledge base, and operates in a short-term, reactive environment where education organizations try to buy and implement change broadly rather than engage in the sustained efforts needed to implement change deeply. (Dolle, Gomez, Russell, Bryk, 2013, p. 445)

When describing the need for improvement science in education, Rohanna (2017) states matter of factly, "Researchers and education practitioners today are still tackling the challenges faced by those 50 years ago, particularly in the area of educational equality" (p. 65). If you examine the outcomes of PK-12 schools, community colleges, and universities, you will no longer wonder if there is a need for improvement.

Educators on all levels have sought improvements with a variety of mechanisms through the years. Policy efforts and grassroots efforts have been aimed at improving one aspect or another of educational systems. Yet the piecemeal efforts have not yielded systemic, widespread results. As educators (and policymakers) try to improve education, you often see two extremes of unfruitful activities—the adding on of interventions that leads to initiative fatigue, or the premature abandonment of interventions that could produce improvements. Cohen and Spillane (1992) stated education reformers are "better at addition than subtraction. They will introduce many different schemes to make education more consistent, but they will be less able to produce consistency among those schemes to greatly reduce the clutter of previous programs and policies, or to fundamentally change teaching" (p. 41). In my own research, K-12 teachers have discussed keeping up with this week's "buzzword" while not really implementing interventions, but just trying to appear as if they are doing so. Initiative fatigue is real, especially when those on the ground charged with implementation know very little about the *why*, but are responsible for the *how*.

On the other hand, because matters of education deal with life outcomes, there is an extreme sense of urgency. As an educator, you do not have time to waste. So, if a program does not seem to be meeting its objectives, it may be time to explore a new or different program. Rohanna (2017) describes an administrator who says educational leaders "tend to adopt, attack, and abandon" (p. 66). Rohanna (2017) goes on to explain that:

> Although school administrators were quick to try a new solution, they were not as adept at improving or modifying a strategy or intervention once it was in place . . . Abandoning potentially effective strategies or interventions before adapting to the specific contexts makes it almost impossible to alleviate the problems facing the education system. (p. 66)

Improvement science has the potential to alleviate the propensity to do each of these—add too much or abandon too quickly. Its deep dive into understanding the system, its stakeholder involvement in the design and implementation of changes, and its rapid tests of an intervention's effectiveness guide practitioners to only adopt or abandon when it makes sense for the organization's predefined goals. While the definitions of improvement science vary—a fact we will explore in the next section—the need is evident. To borrow from *Learning to Improve* (Bryk, Gomez, Grunow & LeMahieu, 2015), *we have to get better at getting better.*

Definitions of Improvement Science

Berwick, a medical doctor and an improvement scientist, described improvement science as a "science of improvement" (2008, p. 1182). But what exactly is the science of improvement? Berwick's description gives you just a preliminary conceptualization. More explicitly, Perla and associates (2013) expound:

> Much of science, especially the applied sciences, has an eye on improving something, yet not all attempts at improving something are scientific. Furthermore, all other sciences focus on a better understanding and improvement of some specific phenomenon that fall within the scope of their discipline (e.g., molecular biology, aviation, food production, education), but the science of improvement is focused on how improvement is done in general. (p. 173)

A science of improvement is the scientific study of how to improve. If you delve into the definitions of *improvement* and *science*, you gain an initial understanding of what improvement science is. Begin with "improvement." In the usual sense of the word, the Oxford English Dictionary defines improvement as "an act of making something better; an instance of becoming better; an addition or alteration by which the quality or standard of something is increased; a change for the better" (OED, 2019). The goal of improvement science is to identify changes or interventions that increase positive outcomes or decrease negative outcomes. Sometimes improvement scientists seek to increase efficiency of processes, or decrease the potency of obstacles, but the aim is to change some part of the system to create an improvement in processes or outcomes. Remember: All improvement requires change, but not all change is improvement!

The second half of the definition is the word "science." The Oxford English Dictionary defines science as "Paired or contrasted with *art* (see ART *n.¹* 3a). A discipline, field of study, or activity concerned with theory rather than method, or requiring the knowledge and systematic application of principles, rather than relying on traditional rules, acquired skill, or intuition" (OED, 2019). It is the science in improvement science that distinguishes it from traditional, and often ineffective, efforts to improve. Improvement science has methodological guidelines, but it provides a framework for how to think critically about problems of practice, and how to guide that thinking to develop a Theory of Improvement (see chapter 6). Furthermore, improvement science requires knowledge (profound knowledge) and the systematic application of the improvement science principles.

In the literature on improvement science, which is not extremely robust since the field is still blossoming, there are different definitions of improvement science (see Table 2.1).

Table 2.1. Scholars' Definitions of Improvement Science

Definition/Description	Source
"Improvement science is about developing, testing, implementing, and spreading **change** informed by subject matter experts. . . improvement science is situated somewhere between change management and research." (Lemire, Christie & Inkelas, 2017, p. 25)	New Directions for Evaluation • Peer-reviewed • Periodical of the American Evaluation Association
"Framing **change** ideas suggested by subject matter experts using a scientific approach in a real-world context is the essence of the science of improvement." (Perla, Provost & Parry, 2013, p. 172)	Quality Management in Health Care • Peer-reviewed

Definition/Description	Source
"A science of improvement offers a productive synthesis. It melds the conceptual and methodological strength associated with scientific study to the contextual specificity, deep clinical insight and practical orientation characteristic of action research. It emphasizes multiple, small rapid tests of **change** by varied individuals working under different conditions. Each test provides a bit of evidence, a bit of local learning. When this activity is organized around causal thinking that links hypothesized solutions to rigorous problem analysis and common data, we accelerate learning for improvement at scale." (Bryk, 2011, para. 4)	EdWeek Blog • Educational news source
"Improvement science . . . is an approach that involves multiple tests of small **changes** that can cumulatively result in larger, system change . . . As an applied science, it emphasizes innovation prototyping, rapid-cycle testing, and spread to generate learning about what changes, in which contexts, produce improvements." (Cohen Vogel, Tichnor-Wagner, Allen, Harrison, Kainz, Socol & Wang, 2015, p. 262)	*Educational Policy* • Peer-reviewed
"Defining features characterizing the science of improvement include cyclical rather than linear approaches, emphasize collaborative over administrative research designs and focus on formative data to guide projects and initiatives [**changes**] . . . improvement science focuses on process variance. Typical improvement work requires a shift in research considerations; where a traditional hypothesis translates into a practical prediction, a random sample becomes a purposive stakeholder group, and a p-value parallels the human side of change." (Crow, 2019, p. 6)	*The Educational Leader's Guide to Improvement Science* • Edited Volume
"Improvement science provides a disciplined approach to learning from practice, by deploying rapid tests of **change** to guide the development, revision and continued fine-tuning of new tools, work processes, roles and norms." (Russell, Bryk, Dolle, Gomez, LeMahieu & Grunow, 2017, p. 17)	*Teachers College Record* • Peer-reviewed

However, despite the differences in definitions, there are key characteristics present in each. Improvement science deals with rapid, iterative tests of change. Remember, all improvement requires change, but all change is *not* an improvement. In three of the six aforementioned, the definition mentions change in context or in a real-world setting. Two definitions also speak to subject matter experts, and that is essential. You must have two types of knowledge, knowledge of the "what" (of what you're trying to improve) *and* knowledge of how to improve, which is where improvement science comes in. Throughout this text, I will use the definition introduced in the beginning, which synthesizes the ones above:

> ***Improvement science*** *is a methodological framework that is under-girded by foundational principles that guide* **scholar-practitioners** *to define problems, understand how the system produces the problems, identify changes to rectify the problems, test the efficacy of those changes, and spread the changes (if the change is indeed an improvement).*

While there are a multitude of definitions within the literature delineating improvement science, "there is general agreement on the ultimate purpose of improvement science, that being continuous improvement through systematic study" (Christie, Lemire & Inkelas, 2017, p. 12). Like all science, the science of improvement is built upon bodies of knowledge and principles that guide its application.

Foundations of Improvement Science: Profound Knowledge, Principles, and Propositions

While improvement science is a blossoming field, it is far from "new." Some argue its roots are in manufacturing in the early 20th century, and it has come of age with its application in business and health care. In this primer's definition, I argue the science of improvement has some undergirding principles and theoretical understandings that drive the process. Different bodies of literature describe these undergirding principles differently, but all agree that Deming's system of profound knowledge is a part of its foundation.

In his book, *The New Economics* (1994), W. E. Deming introduces the four-part *system of profound knowledge*. He stresses, "One need not be eminent in any part nor in all four parts in order to understand it and to apply it" (p. 93). As profound as the knowledge is, anyone (including you or I) can use it. The four parts of the system of profound knowledge are:

- Appreciation for a system
- Knowledge about variation
- Theory of knowledge
- Psychology

Deming defines a system as "a network of interdependent components" that cooperate to try to accomplish some aim (p. 95). He elaborates, "Without an aim, there is no system" (p. 96). You may be thinking about the university system in your state or your school district as a complex system. But if you look on a more molecular scale, your institution, and departments within your institution, down to individual classrooms, are all systems as well. Systems have multiple parts that depend on each other—even your family is a system.

The second facet of profound knowledge is knowledge of variation. Unlike the works of many who write about Deming's work, Deming's work itself is quite approachable. In explaining knowledge of variation, he gives an example of a little girl and her teacher's note to her parents after two tests. On both tests, she scored below average. He goes on to talk about the impact of being told you are below average, and what would happen to self-perception if there was no counternarrative to that message. But what Deming (1994) further points out is, "The teacher failed to observe that roughly half of her pupils will be above average on any test and the other half below . . . there is not much anyone can do about it" (p. 99). This is why we need to understand variation. There is no cause for alarm if half the class is below average; by definition, that is to be expected. Half being above and half being below "average" is predictable, or stable. Not understanding that facet of variation can lead to unnecessary panic and intervention. This is also why measurement is important; the average on some measurement tells us very little. If there is a demarcation for proficiency, and the entire class is above proficient that is excellent, but even in such a case, half would be above average and half below average. Understanding variation helps you identify cause for concern.

The third component of profound knowledge is a theory of knowledge. As stated in a previous section, Deming's ontology is based in prediction: "A statement, if it conveys knowledge, predicts future outcome, with the risk of being wrong, and that it fits without failure observations of the past" (1994, p. 102). He extends his ontological definition, with his epistemological orientation, "Rational prediction requires theory and builds knowledge through systematic revision and extension of theory based on caparison of prediction with observation" (1994, p. 102). In essence, the theory of knowledge is a theory about how one gains knowledge, and according to Deming it is through the testing and revision of theory.

The fourth and final element of profound knowledge is psychology. Deming saw psychology as a means to help managers understand people. He defined management as about prediction, and is known for his 14 points of management in *Out of the Crisis*. He understood that in order to bring about change in an organization, you had to do some work to understand what motivates the people within the organization. He was very critical of ranking individuals, asserting that it only harmed motivation. Since Deming's work, many others have done work on dealing with the human aspect of introducing change. Much of that work is done in the discipline of leadership. Kotter and Schlesinger (1979/2008) give six approaches to managing resistance to change:

- Education and communication
- Participation and involvement
- Facilitation and support
- Negotiation and agreement
- Manipulation and cooptation
- Explicit and implicit coercion

When done with the stakeholders at the table, improvement science has the more positive approaches to managing change embedded in the process.

Langley and associates (2009) speak to the importance of subject matter experts when developing improvements. However, they assert, "The ability to make improvements is enhanced by combining subject matter with profound knowledge in creative ways" (p. 76). You may be an expert on student retention; this primer is not going to supplant that knowledge as you seek to increase your retention rate for first generation students from sophomore year to junior year. Instead, it will show you how to apply that expertise in new ways and help you increase the effectiveness of an intervention your subject matter expertise would lead you to adopt. Hence, in many of the aforementioned definitions, you see the explicit reference to a subject matter expert. To improve, you need subject matter knowledge *and* profound knowledge.

Seven Propositions

Perla, Provost, and Parry (2013) describe seven propositions that are "grounded in the history and philosophy of science" and they "build on each other to define the nature of the science of improvement" (p. 171). Collectively, they define the epistemology of improvement science. The seven propositions are as follows:

1. The science of improvement is grounded in testing and learning cycles.
2. The philosophical foundation of the science of improvement is conceptualistic pragmatism.
3. The science of improvement embraces a combination of psychology and logic (a weak form of psychologism).
4. The science of improvement considers the contexts of justification and discovery.
5. The science of improvement requires the use of operational definitions.

6. The science of improvement employs Shewhart's theory of cause systems.
7. Systems theory directly informs the science of improvement (Perla, Provost & Parry, 2013, p. 171).

Proposition I: Testing, Learning, and Falsification

The first proposition put forth by Perla and associates is the foundation for the interplay between inductive and deductive reasoning within improvement science. The iterative inquiry cycle commonly used, the Plan-Do-Study-Act cycle, is a series of testing and learning and then applying what is learned. Perla and colleagues explain that while many have criticized the improvement methodology as a "lesser way of knowing" because of "the lack of comparison group or randomization" associated with traditional RCTs, it is indeed a science due to the falsification principle espoused by Karl Popper. The falsification principle states any assertion or claim that cannot be tested is not scientific in nature. Jary (2008) explains how Popper advanced the idea that in science, *falsification* was a superior criterion to *verification*:

> According to Popper, given the ever-present possibility of new and potentially refuting evidence, an inductive universal generalization can never be finally verified, whereas a single non-supporting ("falsifying") occurrence can refute a hypothesis. Thus, a single black swan refutes the general hypothesis that "all swans are white." On this view, science is best defined in terms of the "falsifiability," rather than the "verifiability," of its theories and hypotheses. (p. 116)

Falsification is constantly being considered in one of the guiding improvement science questions:

Is the change an improvement? → Yes or No

- Prior to implementing the change, you have determined the threshold for improvement (operationalized what it means to improve). So, you would examine your outcomes against that threshold/goal to decide if an improvement had been made.

If the change *did not* lead to an improvement, does *this* change lead to an improvement? → Yes or No

- You have to determine if the failure was the intervention (change) or failure in the implementation of the change. The change may still lead to an improvement; you just may need to tweak (adjust) your implementation. You must consistently ask yourself whether the change itself is ineffective or if the implementation weakened the potency of the intervention.

After you have evaluated the impacts of implementation, and you find the change itself does not lead to an improvement, you have falsified your theory of improvement. This process shows that falsification is indeed embedded in the science of improvement.

Not everyone agrees falsification is a criterion for science. Some scholars argue that falsification is not the best measure of a theory's merit. Jary (2008) gives the example of Marxism that is difficult falsify, but is still the basis for scientific understanding. He goes on to say in practice, "Falsification often serves well enough as a pragmatic approach" (p. 116).

Proposition II: Conceptualistic Pragmatism

The pragmatic approach is the basis of the second proposition. Perla, Provost, and Parry credit conceptualistic pragmatism as the philosophical foundation of improvement science. Perla and colleagues describe pragmatism as a philosophical shift in focus from "what is 'true' to what is 'useful.'" In this work on the seven propositions, they credit Lewis's *Mind and the New World Order* with influencing Deming and Shewhart, both forerunners of improvement science. Lewis developed conceptualistic pragmatism, which differs slightly from the classical pragmatism discussed in the previous chapter.

Lewis's work on conceptualistic pragmatism was foundational for the epistemology of improvement science. Remember, epistemology deals with how you know what you know and details how knowledge is developed. Lewis's theory said the individual begins with the *a priori*, which Mauléon and Bergman (2009) define as "simply the instrument which our mind imposes upon the sensuously given experience to interpret it" (p. 163). The *a priori* is, in some degree, the theory or schema that already operates within your mind based on your previous experience. Your *a priori* is only changed through the process of reflection. C. I. Lewis posited that knowledge is the result of the interaction between experience and the a priori and "'in this middle ground of trial and error, of expanding experience and the continual shift and modification of conception in our effort to cope with it' that learning takes place" (Mauléon & Bergman, 2009, p. 162). One can see the similarities in Deming's epistemology, where he explains, "Without theory, there is nothing to revise. Without theory, experience has no meaning. Without theory, one has no questions to ask. Hence without theory, there is no learning" (1994, p. 103). An epistemological stance, from conceptualistic pragmatism, supports the initial proposition of the use of testing and learning cycles.

Proposition III: Weak Psychologism

The third proposition states improvement science rests on a form of weak psychologism. If you are not a philosopher, this term may be new for you, and the concept may initially be jarring. Perla and colleagues summarize its relationship to improvement science as, "Provid[ing] the basis for multidisciplinary collaboration and the value of addressing problems from different perspectives" (p. 176). *Psychologism* is the blending of psychology and philosophy (logic).

Cussins (1987) explains, "Both philosophy and psychology are concerned with thought, perception, truth, reference, belief, knowledge, memory, intelligence, etc.," but philosophers are concerned with "thought" while psychologists are more concerned with "thinking" (p. 124–125). Put another way, Cussins (1987) explains that philosophy is concerned with *what* questions, whereas psychology is more concerned with *how* questions. While as an epistemological stance psychologism had a number of critics, Cussins argues for its usefulness, explaining, "A psychologistic doctrine is a doctrine which requires psychology in order to answer a philosophical question" (p. 126).

Perla and associates advocate for a weak form of psychologism. When leading improvement efforts in your college or school, you need to understand the what and the how. Even when the what is a given, you must understand, "People do not always act logically, nor is a 'prescribed' logic necessarily conductive to innovative solutions to complex problems." This is why the quest for "teacher proof" scripted curricula are problematic. Even when mandated with pacing guides and scripted lessons, teachers will adopt to adapt. If we truly want to understand the nature of improvement driven by human behavior, we have to examine both the logic and the psychology that drive choices and decisions of individuals with agency within our organizations.

Proposition IV: Justification and Discovery

There are two major tasks within the improvement science process: discovering or developing improvements and then determining if those improvements actually work. You have to have both in order for your process to be considered improvement science. By the nature of people and their interest, there will be some more excited and involved with discovery phase and other more concerned with the justification phase. Perla, Provost, and Parry (2013) remind their readers that both are equally important, and that the "fundamental contribution of the science of improvement is that it provides a scientific lens to bridge the context of discovery and human experience in the real world and context of justification (using systematic methods and theories)" (p. 179). As improvement science provides that bridge, Perla and associates (2013) caution their readers not to focus too narrowly on one or the other:

> Improvers must always recognize if they are in the "justification" phase of work of the "creative and discovery" phase. Confusing these 2 phases can inhibit the creativity needed to solve problems or minimize the importance of data and measurement. It also reminds us there is usually no single magic bullet solution to a problem and that the cycle of discovery and justification is best viewed as an iterative. (p. 179)

A key part of justification is measurement, and measurement can only be defined once you have a clear understanding of what it means to improve.

Proposition V: Operational Definitions

The fifth proposition may seem like a given. Researchers always begin papers and presentations with definitions. The previous section of this primer is all about definitions. Definitions help get people from different backgrounds on the same page. Improvement teams are often disciplinary, and definitions help pull everyone to the same starting point.

Operational definitions are key to improvement, and key to answering that final improvement science question: How will I know change is an improvement? Deming explained, "An operational definition is a procedure agreed upon for translation of a concept into measurement of some kind" (Deming, 1994, p. 105). Peral, Provost, and Parry (2013) explain it is important to define improvement: "What exactly does it mean to be 'better,' 'more efficient,' 'safer,' 'cost efficient,' etc.?" (p. 179). Throughout this text, you will read a great deal about measurement. When in the midst of an improvement science project, measurement is central to knowing whether or not an improvement has been made. But it is also essential to define what it means to improve.

Propositions VI & VII:
Shewhart's Theory of Cause Systems & Systems Theory

The final two propositions examine theories that inform improvement science. The first one comes from Walter Shewhart, who was Deming's mentor, whose control chart (also referenced as a run chart) is a hallmark tool of improvement science. However, Perla and colleagues make clear, the run chart (discussed in detail in Improvement Science Principle 2) "is more than an applied statistical tool—it is a theory of variation" (p. 180). Shewhart's theory of variation and quest to determine whether processes were in a state of statistical control, was designed to help improvers locate the source (and reason) for variation. In a sense, you have to know what is normal to identify what is abnormal. The theory of variation is a tool to help you understand the processes and outcomes in your organization, prior to making changes. Similarly, the final proposition speaks to the necessity for an understanding of systems theory. As stated earlier, part of Deming's profound knowledge was an appreciation for the system. The explicit use of systems theory is one of many aspects that make improvement science so applicable to education. Systems theory deals with complexity, and educators deal with complex problems of practice.

Perla, Provost, and Parry's propositions provide intellectual and historical foundations of improvement science. Their article on the seven propositions is published in the journal *Quality Management in Health Care*. These propositions describe the nature of improvement science regardless of discipline applying them. However, Bryk, Gomez, Grunow, and LeMahieu's principles, outlined in *Learning to Improve*, illuminate the application of improvement science to problems of practice in education. While I recommend all serious students of the method read and study the propositions, this primer will explore in depth the six principles outlined by Bryk and associates.

The first two chapters in this primer were designed to introduce you to improvement science and distinguish it from traditional educational research. This chapter, specifically, has illustrated the theories that support improvement science being classified as a science. The subsequent chapters will follow the six principles, examining each of them in depth. The first principle, explored in chapter 3, "Collaborating to Define Problems: Definitions with Stakeholder Voices," is the only principle that does not match neatly onto the propositions outlined in this chapter. But this principle, to be user-centered and problem specific, is foundational in using improvement science as a methodological tool for justice.

Key Terms

- **Improvement science**—Improvement science is a methodological framework that is undergirded by foundational principles that guide scholar-practitioners to define problems, understand how the system produces the problems, identify changes to rectify the problems, test the efficacy of those changes, and spread the changes (if the change is indeed an improvement).

- **Psychologism**—Psychologism is the blending of psychology and logic.
- **Scholar practitioner**—A scholar practitioner is a practitioner who guides their practice with scholarship and disciplined inquiry. A scholar practitioner is a reflective practitioner always seeking to improve their organization and their individual practice.
- **System of profound knowledge**—To make improvement in an organization, W. E. Deming said individuals need two types of knowledge: subject matter knowledge and profound knowledge. The system of profound knowledge, weaved throughout the principles of improvement, includes four facets: appreciation for systems, knowledge of variation, a theory of knowledge, and psychology (or knowledge about people).

References

Berwick, D. M. (2008). The science of improvement. *JAMA, 299*(10), 1182–1184.

Bryk, A. (2011, March 31) *It is a science of improvement* [web log comment]. Retrieved from http://blogs.edweek.org/edweek/futures_of_reform/2011/03/it_is_a_science_of_improvement.html

Bryk, A. S., Gomez, L. M., Grunow, A., & LeMahieu, P. G. (2015). *Learning to improve: How America's schools can get better at getting better.* Cambridge, MA: Harvard Education Press.

Christie, C. A., Lemire, S., & Inkelas, M. (2017). Understanding the similarities and distinctions between improvement science and evaluation. *New Directions for Evaluation, 2017*(153), 11–21.

Cohen, D. K., & Spillane, J. P. (1992). Chapter 1: Policy and practice: The relations between governance and instruction. *Review of Research in Education, 18*(1), 3–49.

Cohen-Vogel, L., Tichnor-Wagner, A., Allen, D., Harrison, C., Kainz, K., Socol, A. R., & Wang, Q. (2015). Implementing educational innovations at scale: Transforming researchers into continuous improvement scientists. *Educational Policy, 29*(1), 257–277.

Crow, R. K. (2019) Considering improvement science in educational leadership. In R. Crow, B. Hinnant-Crawford, & D. Spaulding (Eds.*), The educational leader's guide to improvement science: Data, designs, and cases for reflection* (p. 3–12). Gorham, Maine: Myers Education Press.

Cussins, A. (1987). Varieties of psychologism. *Synthese, 70*(1), 123–154.

Deming, W. E. (2000/1986). *Out of the crisis.* Cambridge, MA: MIT Press.

Deming, W. E. (2000/1994). *The new economics for industry, government, education.* Cambridge, MA: MIT Press.

Dolle, J. R., Gomez, L. M., Russell, J. L., & Bryk, A. S. (2013). More than a network: Building professional communities for educational improvement. *National Society for the Study of Education Yearbook, 112*(2), 443-463.

Improvement (2019). Definition 6b. In *Oxford English dictionary*. Retrieved from https://www.oed.com/

Jary, D. (2011) Falsification. In V. Jupp (Ed.), *The SAGE dictionary of social research methods* (116). London: Sage.

Kotter, J. P., & Schlesinger, L. A. (1979/2008). Choosing strategies for change. *Harvard Business Review, 57*(2), 106–114.

Langley, G. J., Moen, R. D., Nolan, K. M., Nolan, T. W., Norman, C. L., & Provost, L. P. (2009). *The improvement guide: A practical approach to enhancing organizational performance.* Hoboken, NJ: John Wiley & Sons.

Lemire, S., Christie, C. A., & Inkelas, M. (2017). The methods and tools of improvement science. *New Directions for Evaluation, 2017*(153), 23–33.

Mauléon, C., & Bergman, B. (2009). Exploring the epistemological origins of Shewhart's and Deming's theory of quality: Influences from CI Lewis' conceptualistic pragmatism. *International Journal of Quality and Service Sciences, 1*(2), 160–171.

National Center for Education Statistics. (2019). *The Condition of Education 2019* (NCES 2019-144). Retrieved from https://nces.ed.gov/pubs2019/2019144.pdf

Perla, R. J., Provost, L. P., & Parry, G. J. (2013). Seven propositions of the science of improvement: Exploring foundations. *Quality Management in Healthcare, 22*(3), 170–186.

Rohanna, K. (2017). Breaking the "adopt, attack, abandon" cycle: A case for improvement science in K–12 education. *New Directions for Evaluation, 2017*(153), 65–77.

Russell, J. L., Bryk, A. S., Dolle, J., Gomez, L. M., LeMahieu, P., & Grunow, A. (2017). A framework for the initiation of networked improvement communities. *Teachers College Record, 119*(7), 1–36.

Science (2019). Definition 4a. In *Oxford English dictionary*. Retrieved from https://www.oed.com/

What Is the Exact Problem I'm Trying to Solve? What Am I Trying to Accomplish?

In *Learning to Improve: How America's Schools Can Get Better at Getting Better*, Bryk, Gomez, Grunow, and LeMahieu (2015) outline six principles of improvement science:

1. Make the work problem-specific and user-centered.
2. Focus on variation in performance.
3. See the system that produces the current outcomes.
4. We cannot improve at scale what we cannot measure.
5. Use disciplined inquiry to drive improvement.
6. Accelerate learning through networked communities (pp. 12–17).

The subsequent chapters in this primer are organized around these six principles and the essential improvement science questions.

Throughout this primer, you will see several questions over and over again. I refer to these questions as **the essential improvement science questions**. These are the guiding questions, identified in Langley and associates' (2009) *Model for Improvement*. Depending on what text you read, *The Improvement Guide, Learning to Improve*, or various articles on improvement science and its applications to education, the wording of the questions differ but the gist remains. The Model for Improvement (MFI) identifies the first question as the aim and it asks, *What are we trying to accomplish?* I often use the question, *What is the exact problem we are trying to solve?* and the follow up, *How do we know the problem is actually a problem?* Whether you look at it as problem identification, or as articulation of the goal, the first set of guiding questions is about the current state and the aspirational state.

While the MFI lays out the questions in a sequential manner, this is not a lockstep process. You can ask these questions at any point in time. However, the first two principles of improvement science as laid out in *Learning to Improve* deal with the questions above— What is the problem and what is the goal? While the semantics are different and they are asking fundamentally different things, these questions ask you to begin by taking stock of where you are so you can decide where you want to be, to paraphrase Septima Clark. The next two chapters examine problems of practice and variance in processes and performance, and give you strategies to understand where you are.

References

Bryk, A. S., Gomez, L. M., Grunow, A., & LeMahieu, P. G. (2015). *Learning to improve: How America's schools can get better at getting better*. Cambridge, MA: Harvard Education Press.

Langley, G. J., Moen, R. D., Nolan, K. M., Nolan, T. W., Norman, C. L., & Provost, L. P. (2009). *The improvement guide: A practical approach to enhancing organizational performance*. Hoboken, NJ: John Wiley & Sons.

CHAPTER THREE

Collaborating to Define Problems

Definitions with Stakeholder Voices

Pragmatists always begin with the question: What works? Improvement scientists are more specific; they ask what works, for whom, and under what circumstances? Critical pragmatists and justice-oriented scholar-practitioners understand they cannot answer these questions alone. Only through a process which intentionally harvests the collective wisdom of many, and synthesizes the prophetic imagination of wide array of stakeholders, can improvement scientists envision better and plot a course for how to get there. Harnessing the power of the collective is the essence of the first principle of improvement science.

In this chapter, I will introduce the first principle of improvement science: Be user-centered and problem specific. At the core of this principle are two questions that guide improvement for equity: *Who is involved?* and *Who is impacted?* In order to define the problem, you have to understand who is impacted; in order to be user-centered, you have to involve those closest to the problem. After defining what it means to be user-centered and problem specific, I will introduce you to tools that will help guide you to make this principle a part of your improvement praxis. Because I am not naïve to the culture and ideology that pervades our educational institutions, I will also make you privy to a common pitfall in the process of problem definition: blaming the victim. This awareness will help you to anticipate and prepare, and to avoid such traps when engaged in improvement science. Lastly, I will introduce you to a final set of tools that can be used to help name problems of practice related to equity.

Naming Problems

Then Jesus demanded, "What is your name?"
—Mark 5:9 (NLT)

To exist, humanly, is to *name* the world, to change it.
Once named, the world in its turn reappears to the namers as a
problem and requires of them a new *naming*.
—Paulo Freire in *Pedagogy of the Oppressed*

In the Christian tradition, when dealing with demonic spirits, the demon is often called by name. In the fifth chapter of the Gospel of Mark, a man suffering demonic possession is described in detail. His growls and moans, his self-mutilation, and his extraordinary strength are all indicators or symptoms of his demonic possession—the root cause. In the way the text is written, knowledge of the symptoms preceded knowledge of the demonic force. To deal with the root cause, there needed to be clear identification of that cause—hence, Jesus raises the question, "What is your name?" Critical pedagogue and literacy scholar Paulo Freire says to name the world is the first step in our quest to change it. To name the problem gives you the power to change it; to name the demon gives you power to cast it out.[1]

---

1   This text is not a theological commentary. Most Christians do not think Christ's ability to cast out demons was contingent upon His asking the name. Those who view Christ as all-knowing would argue He already

Being user-centered and problem specific is how we go about naming problems of practice. This first principal of improvement aligns with the first of the essential improvement science questions: *What is the exact problem I'm trying to solve?* Nebulous problems and poorly defined problems lead to ineffective solutions. Educators tend to be full of solutions and suffer from what Bryk, Gomez, Grunow, and LeMahieu call solutionitis. *Solutionitis* is the tendency for educators to jump to conclusions about the best solution before fully defining the problem. To avoid solutionitis, one must go through systematic steps to define and clarify the problem, and one critical aspect of that process is being user-centered.

Being User-centered

To truly be *user-centered,* one must approach the users, or those closest to the problem, with an asset-based lens. This means, *you cannot see those closest to the problem as the problem.* For example, if you want to improve student outcomes, you cannot assume teachers do not have the students' best interests at heart (even when their instruction is flawed). Berwick warns, "Insensitive suspicion about biases, no matter how well-intended, can feel like attacks on sincerity, honesty, or intelligence" (Berwick, 2008, p. 1184). You need information from the users, and you will not get it if they are offended at the beginning of the discussions about defining the problem.

As with all research, when engaging in improvement work, you have to be aware of power dynamics. Moreover, you cannot view the user as solely a source of information and not a vital part of the, yet to be revealed, solution. You should try to recognize, *and appreciate,* all of what the user brings to the table. To be an improvement scientist, you cannot be guided by a deficit ideology. *Deficit Ideology* is a worldview that rationalizes and justifies inequalities in outcomes

---

knew the name. But Christ's behavior was always intentional as to set an example for his disciples and followers—who would not possess the knowledge He had.

and locates the cause of those outcomes within the very communities whose outcomes you are trying to improve. While I give the example of a deficit perspective of teachers above, deficit ideology is common stance in those from traditionally and historically marginalized communities. Deficit perspectives are prevalent in elementary, secondary, and post-secondary education. Ladson-Billings (2007) outlines five common assertions in PK-12 education, that are rooted in deficit understandings of students and their communities:

- The parents just don't care.
- These children don't have enough exposure/experiences.
- These children aren't ready for school.
- Their families don't value education.
- They are coming from a culture of poverty. (p. 317)

Ladson-Billings goes on to debunk each one of these myths, rooted in deficit ideology, that plague educators' common sense. Paul Gorski, of edchange.org, explains the most insidious aspect of deficit ideology is that it "discounts sociopolitical context, such as the systematic conditions (racism, economic injustice, and so on) that grant some people greater social, political, and economic access, such as that to high-quality schooling, than others" (Gorski, 2011, p. 153). Bensimon (2005) characterizes deficit ideology as a deficit cognitive frame, and she gives examples of how deficit ideology plays out in higher education, where concepts such as diversity and inclusion are explicitly valued. She explains:

> Individuals with a deficit cognitive frame may value diversity and have positive attitudes toward increasing minority student participation in higher education, but they are inclined to attribute differences in educational outcomes for Black, Hispanic, and Native American students, such as lower rates of retention or degree completion, to cultural stereotypes, inadequate socialization, or lack of motivation and initiative on the part of the students . . . It can also be conveyed in well-meaning but pessimistic attributions, such as concluding that students cannot be expected to overcome the disadvantages of poverty and under preparation; therefore, unequal outcomes are to be expected. (p. 102)

If you get to a point where you believe disparate outcomes are *fait accompli,* you will doubt the possibility or neglect to see the necessity of improving such outcomes. Deficit ideology is a dangerous obstacle for improvement work. Furthermore, if you locate the problem in the user, you neglect to see the failure of the system, which will lead you to trying to change people instead of improving the system.

To avoid deficit ideology's derailing your problem definition process, there are a few things you can do:

1. *Be prepared.* Know what the common deficit laden assumptions that may be held among the folks on your improvement team.

2. *Do your research and bring data and/or literature that combats commonly held deficit views.* In an initial meeting, you may begin with some common understandings about the population you are serving (first generation college students, English language learners, African American boys, etc.). You may create a slide presentation or a one-page handout with myths versus facts, so everyone in your team begins on the same page. As you compile resources, books like *Is Everybody Really Equal?: An Introduction to Key Concepts in Social Justice Education* by Ozlem Sensoy and Robin DiAngelo (Teachers College Press) can be a useful resource. As the improvement champion, be willing to do some prework, and begin by educating your team. Ideology does not change overnight; however, anticipate (and be prepared for) teachable moments related to deficit ideology.

3. *Teach; Do not police.* As people are changing and learning—do not be so much of an expert that you turn them off—this is especially the case when it comes to terminology and language. For example, if you are teaching your team to use person-first language and someone describes someone as "autistic," do not inadvertently mute their contribution because you are too focused on correction. Similarly, do not assume a shift in terminology is a shift in understanding. For example, if the team starts saying "opportunity gap" instead of "achievement gap."

4. *Be willing to proceed without conceding.* Everyone may not
   buy into an asset-based view of the community you are serving.
   Teachers who began their careers believing that Ruby Payne's
   framework for poverty was the gospel may have a difficult time
   seeing an asset view of impoverished students. Use the moment to teach about deficit ideology and why it is problematic,
   but move forward even if all members of the team have not
   fully embraced a new world view (expect some pushback). One
   way to move them forward even when there is a lack of consen-
   sus is to remind the team to focus on what is in your sphere of
   influence. Redirecting the team to focus on what you actually
   have control over should move their attention from blaming
   students and their communities for systemic problems. Also,
   do not feel defeated if everyone is not on board. You have plant-
   ed a seed. Never underestimate the power of planting seeds.

Related to deficit ideology is respecting the users you invite
to the table. In an effort to do no harm, do not invite users to be
a part of your process for defining problems if you cannot respect
and appreciate what they bring to the table. Being user-centered
requires humility on the part of the improvement scientists and
improvement teams. You may possess knowledge about testing
change, but users possess knowledge about processes and contexts
that you may not have access to. And when there is a power differential, you are the principal and the users are teachers, or you are a
professor and the users are students, or you are a district employee
and the users are parents, be explicit that you honor their knowledge and expertise and that you cannot do the work you are trying
to do without their help. As Bryk and associates explain:

> At its most basic level, being user centered means respecting the
> people who actually do the work by seeking to understand the
> problems they confront. It means engaging these people in design-
> ing changes that align with the problems they really experience.
> (2015, p. 32)

When we operate from a deficit frame, we cannot be user-centered.

Defining the Problem

The process of problem definition seems simple at first. However, usually when we recognize a problem, what we see first is the symptom of the problem, not the problem itself. So, it is essential to look beyond the symptom to determine the actual underlying cause of the problem. Root Cause Analysis (RCA) is a process used to clearly define problems of practice. Root cause analysis helps to answer the first improvement science question: *What is the exact problem I am trying to solve?* To determine root causes, you have to look below the surface, at the "roots" of the tree, to determine what is truly the cause of the problem. In complex organizations or systems, you need individuals who view the problem from various perspectives. Therefore, you need individuals who represent different parts of the organization for the most comprehensive view of the problem. This includes those closest to the problem as well as those who have a bird's eye view of the entire system, usually those in leadership. As the improvement scientist, you have to be aware that some people will come to the task of root cause analysis with a deficit perspective, and you have to be ready to address that when it arises. If you know there are commonly held deficit beliefs about the problem or the users, you may want to address them at the beginning of your convening.

You also have to be prepared to account for power differentials among the stakeholders in the room, in order to get the most accurate information. It may be necessary for you to gather different groups of stakeholders at different times, using the logic behind segmentation with focus groups (Morgan, 1996). For example, if junior (untenured) faculty believe the dean of the college's decisions are the root cause of some problem, they are not likely to say that in front of the dean, for fear of repercussions. As you employ improvement science, do not neglect what you know about human nature.

Once you have the right people at the table, you are ready to undertake a systematic process of defining the problem. There are multiple approaches to RCA. One is outlined in detail in *Problem Solving 101: The Little Book for Smart People* (Wantanabe, 2009).

Recommended Addition for the Improvement Scientist's Bookshelf

In *Problem Solving 101,* the author lists two steps in problem solving. Step 1, "diagnose the situation and identify the root cause of the problem," is divided into four sub-steps:

1. List all the potential causes of the problem.
2. Develop a hypothesis for the likely root cause.
3. Determine the analysis and information required to test the hypothesis.
4. Analyze and identify the root cause.

While it may seem simple, problem definition can be complex.

Tools for Root Cause Analysis

The Five Whys

There are a number of tools for root cause analysis. If you Google "root cause analysis," it returns 208,000,000 hits in less than a second. I will introduce two methods of root cause analysis here, but there are many more out there waiting for your exploration. The first method has been widely used by engineering professionals and it is the Five Whys Technique. The Five Whys was developed by Sakichi Toyoda while working for Toyota (Serrat, 2017). This technique examines a problem by asking why it is happening five times. The first step is identifying and articulating a clear problem. Suppose you and your honey are experiencing relationship problems. Your inclination is to blame your honey for not being as sweet as they once were, but the Five Whys leads you to another conclusion. You begin with the problem:

Problem: The spark is gone.

🔍 **Why?**
    🐟 We've grown apart.
🔍 **Why?**
    🐟 We don't spend a lot of time together.
🔍 **Why?**
    🐟 I work a lot.
🔍 **Why?**
    🐟 My job has increased its demands.
🔍 **Why?**
    🐟 Layoffs

Now, you realize your sweetie is not the reason the flame is gone, but the changes in your work demands have introduced a strain on your relationship. The same approach can be applied to a problem of practice within the realm of education.

When using Five Whys and other RCA techniques, you have to be aware that deficit perspectives can creep in. For example, this same series yields different results if in your heart your sweetie was the cause.

Problem: The spark is gone.

🔍 **Why?**
    🐟 We've grown apart.
🔍 **Why?**
    🐟 We don't spend a lot of time together
🔍 **Why?**
    🐟 Sweetie always has an attitude.
🔍 **Why?**
    🐟 Because Sweetie is moody.
🔍 **Why?**
    🐟 Because Sweetie is selfish and always has to have things their way.

While this is a silly example, it further illustrates the importance of having multiple perspectives at the table when completing RCAs. If Sweetie was at the table, this would not be the agreed upon root cause. However, if you completed this with your mother and your best friend (who can be presumed to be on your side), you might end up with a root cause that is grounded in a deficit view of your honey.

The Five Whys is lauded as an RCA technique for its simplicity and its pedigree, being born out of the Toyota Production System. However, it is not without its critiques. Scholars argue you can use more or less than five whys, and some say this technique should be used in conjunction with other techniques, not as a stand-alone approach to RCA. Card (2016) argues the Five Whys technique "forces users down a single analytical pathway for any given problem, insists on a single root cause as the target for solutions, and assumes that the most distal link on the causal pathway (the fifth 'why') is inherently the most effective and efficient place to intervene" (p. 2). In fact, Card (2016) suggests the use of more systems-oriented techniques such as the fishbone diagram.

The Fishbone Diagram

The *fishbone diagram, or Ishikawa diagram*, was created by Karou Ishikawa as a tool to advance quality control, and was informed by the work of Tamiko Hashimoto. In his text, *Guide to Quality Control*, Ishikawa (1986) refers to the diagram as a cause-and-effect diagram. He gives three general steps for making a cause-and-effect diagram:

1. Determining the quality characteristic you want to improve (the problem)
2. Identifying the major factors causing it
3. Identifying the detailed factors that may contribute to the broader factors, what he described as "twigs"

For this example, pretend you are the principal at a predominately Black and Latinx elementary school; however, your teaching staff is 93% White. You have been reading literature that says the outcomes for students of color improve if they have even one teacher from their racial background within their K-12 career. Your problem is, your teachers do not reflect the identities of your students. You assemble a team to examine why this problem exists, and you use the fishbone diagram to help scaffold your thinking.

Figure 3.1. Head of a Fishbone Diagram

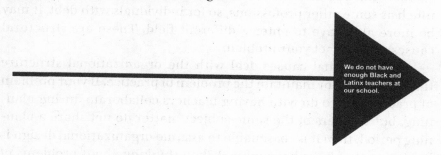

We do not have enough Black and Latinx teachers at our school.

Initially, when Ishikawa created the diagram, he used anchors or "major possible causal factors" such as "raw materials (materials), equipment (machines or tools), method of work (workers), measuring method (inspection)" to illuminate the diversity and categories of root causes that could impact a manufacturing or production problem. In education, the root cause categories may be different, but as you develop your fishbone diagram you may think about some of the following:

- Structural causes
- Organizational causes
- Policy causes
- Ideological causes
- Capacity causes
- Historical causes
- Resource causes
- Practice/Pedagogical causes

Unlike Ishikawa's distinct categories, like man and materials, the ones listed above may overlap and be interrelated. Structural causes tend to include societal systems that are difficult for you to manipulate. They also include large wicked problems such as poverty, racism, sexism, ableism, xenophobia, heterosexism, and ageism. In this case, you may think about the resources of prospective teachers of color and you may recognize that Black and Latinx individuals in the United States are more likely to be impoverished. Therefore, they are less likely to go to college without having to take on debt. You also know that teaching as a profession does not pay as much as some other professions, so for individuals with debt, it may be more attractive to enter a different field. These are structural causes that impact your problem.

Organizational causes deal with the organizational structure that may create or maintain the problem of practice. If your problem of practice has to do with having teachers collaborate during planning, but teachers of the same subject matter do not share a planning period, then it is reasonable to assume organizational design is hindering that from happening. When thinking about problems of practice, you have to be intentional about seeing the entire system (which we discuss more in the following chapters).

Policy is made at multiple levels: federal, state, local, institutional, and departmental. So, when you think about policy, do not say X federal statute makes it impossible to do anything to address this problem. This is an excuse. Policies higher up are usually broader, and it is the local or institutional policy that dictates how the policy plays out on the ground. For example, your state's licensure policy requires teachers to pass several exams for certification. But your local college requires prospective teacher education students to pass the exam prior to admission to the major. You would have to ask whether this gatekeeping exam effectively reduces the number of students of color who go into the major. How is this policy impacting your outcome?

Ideological causes are often skirted by some educators. Educators like to argue that they are neutral, despite Paulo Freire's declaration that education is never neutral. Deficit ideology can be the root cause of some outcomes. There is also sometimes a question of will. You have to ask the obvious: Is recruiting teachers of color a priority for the administrators? And if your answer is no, you think about whether or not making it an administrative priority is central to solving your problem of practice. If it is, then you have to think about how to shift their thinking about the benefits of a diverse teaching staff.

Capacity causes are often part of the educational problems of practice, and are typically some of the first improvement scientist seek to address. Capacity is the ability for an organization or an individual to complete a task or fulfill are particular mission. As educators define problems of practice, it may become evident that team members or structures and systems do not have the expertise or bandwidth to make certain goals happen. When defining school capacity in the K-12 setting, Newmann, King, and Youngs (2000) said you have to consider five things: "teacher knowledge, skills, and dispositions; professional community; program coherence; technical resources; and principal leadership" (p. 259). Capacity root causes are usually addressed with some type of professional learning or coaching intervention; educators are comfortable and confident in their ability to build capacity. In this example, you may think about your school and/or district's capacity to recruit diverse teachers.

You cannot take an ahistorical stance in your analysis of problems of practice. Are there historical events or historical barriers that have led to the problem we are encountering? In the case of teachers of color, you have to consider the widescale firing of Black teachers and leaders in the South during the process of integration. How has that historical practice impacted the pipeline? How does not seeing Black teachers impact Black children's desire to become teachers?

Often educators are faced with limited resources. Resource constraints are often a cause of some problems we face. However, when you consider the myriad factors leading to your problem, even when you do not have the resources (fiscal or human), you find there are other factors you can do something about. Also, when you are explicit about the resource constraints, you can find creative ways to ameliorate that resource gap. So, it is important to include resources as well.

While educators often use the language of best practice and they try to employ best practice, sometimes it is our practice that leads to our outcomes. As you move away from a deficit perspective, you must examine internal practices or behaviors that may contribute to the problem you see. This also requires you to be user-centered and accommodate multiple voices at the table. Sometimes you will not be able to see how your practice contributes to the problem, whereas it may be evident to others.

Remember, your fishbone does not have to consist of only these factors, but as you examine and refine your diagram (which will be a living document), you want to ensure you have considered these as well.

Ishikawa (1986) states it is critical that "group members must speak openly with one another to adequately construct cause and effect diagrams" (p. 20). In doing this root cause analysis and constructing this fishbone diagram, you should have several individuals at the table. With the present problem of practice, a lack of teachers of color at your elementary school, your thought partners should include (at a minimum): someone from human resources, someone from education preparation, and Black and Latinx teachers and paraprofessionals. Your initial discussion leads you to four causes you want to further explore: hiring, salaries, priorities, and retention.

Figure 3.2. Major Branches on a Fishbone Diagram

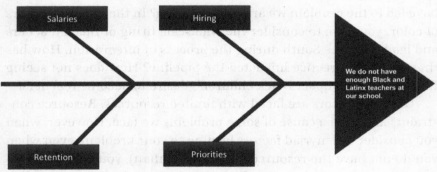

You can use the Five Whys to help you flesh out each of the major branches on your tree. The Five Whys technique works well for determining what should be included in the fishbone. If we examined the role of hiring on our non-diverse teaching force, using the Five Whys, it might look something like this:

Figure 3.3. Using the Five Whys Technique to Inform Your Fishbone

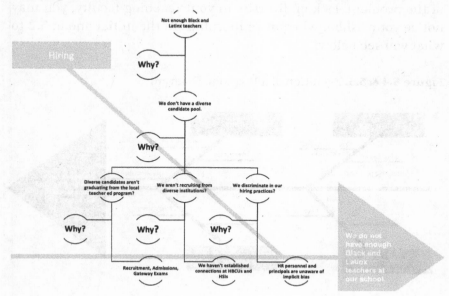

Note, you do not have to use these techniques simultaneously or superimpose the Five Whys onto the fishbone. This is for illustration purposes only. The example above only shows three whys, but in your own investigation, you would continue to drill down or stop where you feel appropriate.

Ishikawa (1986) warns that if your fishbone is too simplistic, as is illustrated in Figure 3.2, then "either your knowledge of the ... process is too shallow or the diagram is too generalized" (p. 29). Ishikawa also is explicit about the various uses for the diagram. He explains it is a tool for learning and that "everyone taking part in making this diagram will gain new knowledge" (p. 25). In this case, it is often important for political reasons to have various leadership involved so their understanding of the problem will grow, and they will be ready to endorse subsequent proposed changes. Ishikawa also said the diagram can be a tool for discussion and used for any problem. The reason you should use it in improvement science is that "The aim is to get results; knowing the relationship between cause and effect will lead to a quicker solution" (Ishikawa, 1986, p. 28).

After several meetings and research about the potential causes of the problem, lack of diversity in your teaching faculty, you may notice your fishbone begins to morph from the initial one in 3.2 to what you see below:

Figure 3.4 & 3.5. Evolution of a Fishbone Diagram

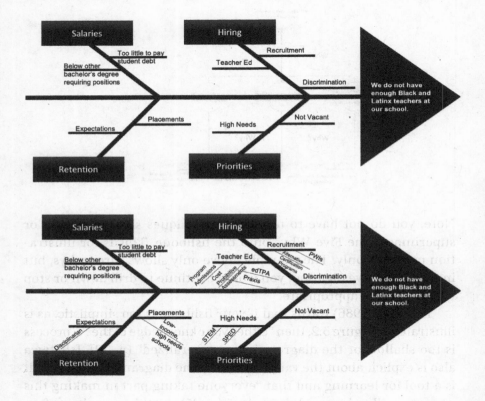

As you continue on this journey, you realize that what you thought was initially a pipeline issue is much more complex than that. As you explored hiring, questions arose about why your district does not intentionally recruit from historically black colleges and universities and Hispanic-serving institutions. Your reading of research and examination of district data shows that teachers of color, particularly Black teachers, tend to be placed in the schools with the highest needs (D'amico, Pawlewicz, Earley & McGeehan, 2017), and there are unwritten expectations that these teachers will serve as disciplinarians. There is also data that show teachers of color are discriminated against in the hiring process (D'amico et al., 2017). When you examine organizational priorities by talking with various leaders, you see they placed an emphasis on hiring STEM and special education teachers and stated there are no job vacancies directed toward teachers from underrepresented backgrounds. And while low salaries affect teachers across the board, regardless of their racial or ethnic backgrounds, the amount of debt one has after college may impact their decision to go in the field, and graduates of color have disproportionately more debt (Huelsman, 2015). As you examine your completed fishbone, you may see evidence of the types of root causes discussed below, even if they do not serve as your anchors.

Figure 3.6. Fishbone and Types of Educational Root Causes

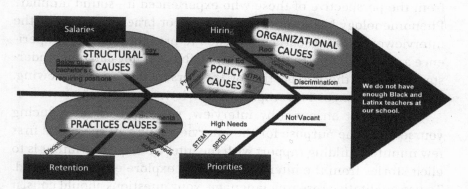

Empathy Interviews

The final tool I will introduce to aid in problem definition simultaneously aids in your ability to be user-centered and to understand the problem from the user's perspective. While I introduce it here, it is also a tool for design thinking, which is discussed in chapter 6. *Empathy interviews* are a data collection strategy that seeks to understand some concept or experience from the perspective of the interviewee. This tool can be especially useful if you think power dynamics will mute some voices when you get all stakeholders around the table. This technique could add an element of confidentiality or anonymity depending on who conducts the interview, that will help to disguise the voices of the vulnerable, but still have them present in the room. It is always best to have diverse voices in the room, and empathy interviews should not be seen as a substitute for including diverse voices.

Empathy interviews can be used for a variety of purposes: problem definition, system exploration, and data collection on processes or outcomes. For example, if you are a teacher seeking to study a new curriculum from the perspective of the student, you might conduct interviews with students who have experienced that particular curriculum. People often think of empathy interviews as hallmark of design thinking; the truth is they can also be traced to ethnographic and phenomenological research. Ethnographies seek to study culture, and phenomenologies seek to study phenomena from the perspective of those who experienced it—sound familiar? Phenomenology has a concept of epoche, or bracketing, where the interviewer or the researcher is asked to bracket their own experience and knowledge, to the extent possible, so they can only understand it from the perspective of the person they're interviewing. This is the essence of an empathy interview.

To conduct an empathy interview, you begin by introducing yourself and the purpose for the interview, and you spend the first few minutes building rapport with the interviewee. Your intent is to elicit stories from the interviewee and to explore emotions shared. To use qualitative research language, your questions should consist primarily of open-ended main questions. Rubin and Rubin (2005) explain main questions are "broad questions that are relatively easy to answer from the interviewee's experience" (p. 157). To understand the system, processes, or the problem from the perspective of a user (teacher, professor, student, parent, psychologist, student affairs professional, HR director, etc.), you may want to begin with tour questions. A tour question is one "in which you suggest to your interviewee to act more or less as guides, walking you through their turf while pointing out what they think is important on the way" (Rubin

& Rubin, 2005, pp. 159–160). Questions like, "What is a typical day like in your classroom?" gives a teacher or student free range to acknowledge what they see as the most important aspects of what happens in the class. Empathy interviews can yield a lot of information quickly. When choosing who to interview, you should choose individuals who are experienced (firsthand experience of whatever you are exploring) and knowledgeable. You want to interview individuals from a variety of perspectives (Rubin & Rubin, 2005).

The main thing to remember with an empathy interview is to remove yourself—your knowledge and your biases, so you can truly listen to the interviewee and understand their perspective of the phenomenon in question.

Five Whys, fishbone diagrams, and empathy interviews are tools that can aid you in understanding, defining, and naming problems of practice. Each of these tools suggests you have some initial understanding, based on outcomes or symptoms, that a problem actually exists. The next section offers tools to help you identify problems of practice related to equity.

Tools for Identifying Problems Related to Educational Equity

Equity Audits

Some educational problems are in your face and they cannot be overlooked; others may go under your radar if you are not explicitly looking for them. Before you can address a problem, you have to identify that one exists. *Equity audits* are tools to help you uncover where inequities within your school may exist. Equity audits, also referred to as representivity audits, have "a deep and significant history in civil rights enforcement" (Skrla, Scheurich, Garcia & Nolly, 2004, p. 138) and are gaining traction as a tool for educators to disrupt inequities. There are a variety of equity audits within the academic literature for you to use to explore equity-focused problems of practice within your school or district (Green, 2017; Fraturra & Capper, 2007; Groenke, 2010; Skrla et al., 2004). This chapter will highlight some of them and direct you to resources if you choose to use this inquiry method as a part of your improvement science process.

Equity audits are a useful and practical tool in defining educational problems. Skrla and associates (2004) explain:

> For teachers and administrators to have a more productive orientation, one that is not deficit based or focused on issues external to schools, they need to be assisted in recognizing that there are substantial and persistent patterns of inequity internal to schools (i.e., embedded within the many assumptions, beliefs, practices, procedures, and policies of schools themselves) . . . our reconception of equity audits is intended to facilitate ease of use and to promote insight into, discussion of, and a substantive response to systemic patterns of inequity in schools and school districts. (p. 141)

Their tool helps to determine equity across three dimensions: equity in teacher quality, equity in programmatic access, and equity in achievement. They espouse the belief that ensuring teacher quality, achievement equity, and programmatic equity will lead to equitable outcomes.

Figure 3.7. Equity Audit's Logic for Achieving Equity

In terms of teacher quality, Skrla and colleagues suggest it is incumbent upon equity advocates to ensure equitable distribution of teachers with regard to their level of education (advanced degrees), experience, mobility, and certification status. Lankford, Loeb, and Wyckoff (2002) have documented the inequitable distribution of teachers, and the Harvard Strategic Data Project has developed tools for helping districts determine if the neediest students have access to the highest quality teachers.

The second-dimension of the Skrla et al. (2004) equity audit deals with programmatic equity. There are four subcomponents to programmatic equity: special education, gifted education, bilingual education, and discipline. Scholars (Ford, 1998; Harry & Klinger, 2014; Rush & Robinson, 2019) have long documented the overrepresentation of students of color in special education and the underrepresentation in gifted education. Bilingual education is described as sometimes being a "language ghetto," and of subpar quality, which disadvantages linguistically diverse populations. Last but not least, discipline is a part of the programmatic dimension, because exclusionary discipline practices detract from students' opportunities to learn.

The final dimension in this equity audit is achievement equity. It is critically important not to use a single measure of achievement. Skrla, Scheurich, Garcia, and Nolly (2004) suggest using state exam data, dropout and graduation rates, high school tracks (i.e., standard, honors, college-preparatory, AP), and collegiate entrance exam and advanced placement scores. While studying outcome data is ostensibly straightforward, embedded within the equity audit is the idea if the outcomes are not equitable, perhaps the schooling process is not equitable. Tracking operates much like special education. Oakes (1986) explains:

> Despite meritocratic justifications and democratic intent, these data show an unequal distribution of learning opportunities in a direction that favors the already privileged. In the name of equal opportunity, track levels I schools, reflective of social and economic groupings in society, are provided with differential access to school opportunities that is likely to maintain or increase, rather than erase the inequities in the larger social structure. (p. 63)

Knowing the distribution of various student groups in each track is critical for understanding equity in your school/district.

Collectively, examining teacher quality, programmatic access, and achievement outcomes can give you a sense of where there are areas for improvement. Finally, Skrla and colleagues (2004) suggest as process for conducting an equity audit: 1) convene a team of stakeholders, 2) present the data and have the team graph the data, 3) discuss what it means, 4) generate solutions, 5) implement solutions, and 6) monitor results. Finally, either celebrate or return to step 3 and repeat the process. As in improvement science, they suggest an iterative process.

Frattura and Capper's (2007) equity audit has more dimensions and prompts for thinking about the data. Their audit, which is found in Appendix B of the book, *Leadership for Social Justice*, includes the following domains: general and social class data and analysis, status of labeling at your school, discipline data, general achievement data, social class, race and ethnicity data and analysis, English language learners and bilingual data and analysis, (dis)ability data and analysis, gender data and analysis, and finally, sexual orientation and gender identity data and analysis (pp. 239–246). Equity audits are about access. Disaggregating data will reveal who has access to what in your school or building. You may choose to disaggregate in terms of race, linguistic background, socioeconomic status, migrant status, gender, and/or sexuality (which will be more difficult until it is a consistent data marker in data management systems). But it is about getting you to see what is happening in a concrete way.

Terrence Green (2017) advances the idea of Community-Based Equity Audits for school leaders to work in solidarity with school communities to advance community-school improvements. Community-Based Equity Audits do not proceed in a linear fashion or with in-sync steps, but can be adapted to meet the needs of each situation. There are four phases of the Community-Based Equity Audit: 1) disrupting deficit views of the community, 2) conducting initial community inquiry and shared experiences, 3) developing a community leadership team, and 4) collecting equity, asset-based data for action (Green, 2017, p. 17). Depending on your problem of practice, the Community-Based Equity Audit can be a useful process in helping your team to be user-centered.

Diversity & Inclusive Excellence Scorecards

The equity audits discussed above are geared toward PK–12 educational institutions, but similar tools are employed in higher education settings. Like equity audits in the elementary and secondary educational arena, the *Diversity Scorecard* in higher education is a tool that is designed to help educators "see, on their own, and as clearly as possible, the magnitude of inequities (awareness). They then must analyze and integrate the meaning of these inequities (interpretation), so that they are moved to act upon them (action)" (Bensimon, 2004, p. 46). Similarly, the Inclusive Excellence Scorecard is described as a "tool [that] allows campuses to pinpoint where they are doing well and where they need improvement on a set of Inclusive Excellence goals" (Williams, Berger & McClendon, 2005, p. 19). In the case of equity audits and the scorecards, the goal is not simply to illuminate disparities, but to bring awareness of what inequities exist within the organization so that they can be addressed. The purpose of these tools is not to fetishize gaps in any particular domain but to illustrate student populations that may be underserved.

The Diversity Scorecard and the Inclusive Excellence Scorecard are set up like the Balanced Scorecard, which came from the business world. The Balanced Scorecard, introduced by Kaplan and Norton in the early 1990s, was developed around four main questions:

1. How do our customers see us? (customer perspective)
2. What must we excel at? (internal perspective)
3. Can we continue to improve and create value? (innovation/ learning perspective)
4. How do we look to our shareholders? (financial perspective)

Instead of focusing solely on the bottom line, which was dominated by lagging variables, the Balanced Scorecard provided a more holistic view of businesses and included indicators that could predict future success. Each question or perspective had goals and indicators to determine whether a company was making progress toward those goals. While the Balanced Scorecard has been used in education, often, the bottom line is student achievement.

Like the Balanced Scorecard, the Diversity Scorecard has four perspectives: the access perspective, the retention perspective, the institutional receptivity perspective, and the excellence perspective

(Bensimone, 2004). It is important to note that the Diversity Scorecard has been used in two-year, four-year, private and public institutions (Bensimon, 2004). The access perspective determines the extent to which underrepresented populations have access to the institution: its programs and its resources. The retention perspective examines disaggregated data on retention and persistence from semester to semester and from year to year. The retention perspective would also examine the completion of basic skills courses, degree, and/or certificate programs. The institutional receptivity perspective examines the campus environment, particularly with regards to human capital on campus. Bensimon explains this perspective answers questions such as: "Do new hires at the institution enhance the racial and ethnic diversity of the faculty, administrators, and staff? Does the composition of the faculty correspond to the racial and ethnic composition of the body?" (2004, p. 47). The last perspective included is the excellence perspective; instead of simply examining completion, this perspective investigates the percentage of underrepresented students graduating with a 3.5 or above grade point average and examines the completion rates for students in highly competitive programs.

Like the equity audit, the building of the diversity scorecard is a process. Step one is to disaggregate basic data and create a "diversity vital signs profile," which includes enrollment data by major/program, persistence rates, GPA distributions, and financial aid by award type (Bensimon, 2004, p. 48). Bensimon's scorecard looked primarily at race and ethnicity, but you could also disaggregate data according to Pell eligibility, veteran status, (dis)ability status, first generation status, online vs. residential students, non-traditional students, and other indicators your institution may track. To be clear, while you may want to examine other indicators, you should not fail to include race and ethnicity. Bensimon explains while institutions track data like enrollment and persistence regularly, "they rarely disaggregate data on student outcomes" (p. 48). Step one in developing the scorecard is to establish your baseline for various student populations on campus in each of the perspectives.

The second step is defining goals in each area. After you have examined the data, you have to operationalize what improvement is, and determine how you will know when you have made improvement. Bensimon does not consider the development of a Diversity Scorecard as a data collection activity that precedes an intervention; she articulates that the development of the scorecard *is*, in itself, the intervention. She maintains that the "aim is for team members to gain deep understanding of inequities in educational outcomes by actively creating the tools that lead to their own recognition of the problem and their subsequent commitment to address it" (p. 52).

The last and final step of the Diversity Scorecard is to share it with campus stakeholders.

Similar to the Diversity Scorecard, the Inclusive Excellence Scorecard is a multidimensional measurement tool that helps institutions of higher education (IHEs) define and track their progress toward inclusive excellence. Williams, Berger, and McClendon (2005) defined *inclusive excellence* for the American Association of Colleges and University as an understanding that "diversity is a key component of a comprehensive strategy for achieving institutional excellence—which includes, but is not limited to, the academic excellence of all students in attendance and concerted efforts to educate all students to succeed in a diverse society and equip them with sophisticated intercultural skills" (2005, p. 3). While similar in nature, the Inclusive Excellence Scorecard examines different dimensions than the Diversity Scorecard, looking closely at collegiate inputs in addition to outcomes. The four dimensions of an Inclusive Excellence Scorecard include: access and equity, campus climate, curricular diversity, and learning and development.

The first dimension, access and equity, combines the access and retention dimensions of the Diversity Scorecard. In this dimension, you could use enrollment and/or employment data to view the incidence of underrepresented individuals on campus (students, staff, faculty, and administrators). However, if using this tool, you would not stop at aggregate figures of incidence. With inclusive excellence, you would also examine incidence of diversity by program/major for students and by status for faculty (such as representation of minoritized faculty at the assistant, associate, and full professor rank).

With one of the goals of inclusive excellence focusing on what students have a chance to learn, this scorecard also looks at the diverse voices and perspectives represented in curricula and the opportunity for all students to increase their intercultural knowledge. Indicators you could include regarding formal and informal curriculum are: the quantity of courses offered that are focused on intercultural subject matter as well as the number of lectures or cultural events on campus.

The campus climate dimension of the Inclusive Excellence Scorecard may use traditional survey measures of student perceptions of campus climate. It examines whether the sense of belonging is consistent across different groups of students. In addition to survey data on climate, IHEs may also examine incidence of harassment based on racisms, sexisms, or heterosexism as an indicator of the campus climate. The fourth and final dimension deals with student outcomes. While the second dimension focuses on opportunity to develop intercultural competence, the final dimension examines evidence of growth in intercultural competence.

Both the Diversity Scorecard and the Inclusive Excellence Scorecard can be useful in defining problems of practice related to equity in IHEs. Scorecards help you determine your baseline, like equity audits. They require you to slice and dice your data, so areas of weakness become visible. When the problem is clear, you can name it, identify it, and then begin the process of resolving it.

Defining Problems with Stakeholder Voices

Problem definition is often overlooked when trying to improve in education. As a profession filled with altruistic, well-intentioned individuals, educators jump to conclusions about solutions before they identify the problem. If improvement efforts are to be effective, that has to stop. We must delve deeper into problems of practice and identify root causes. The Five Whys, the fishbone diagram, and empathy interviews are approaches to help you or your team systematically examine what you think underlies the problem you are trying to address.

Some organizations like to assert that equity issues do not exist within their systems, especially when their systems are racially homogeneous, or lacking in racial diversity. When examining issues of equity, it is important to look closely at all types of diversity to make sure no demographic is underserved. Equity audits, Diversity Scorecards, and Inclusive Excellence Scorecards are tools to help illuminate blind spots. Biag (2019) challenges improvement scientists and scholar-practitioners to navigate the improvement journey with an "equity compass." He outlines three principles to do this: 1) practice critical reflection through an equity lens, 2) promote inclusion, and 3) focus on the whole child (Biag, 2019). The first two principles are fundamental in defining problems and being user-centered. It is critical to reflect and see whether your assumptions and those of your improvement teams are based in deficit understandings. To understand the problem from the user's experience, it is necessary to have a variety of voices at the table. You have to be humble. You have to listen.

After you have identified the problem and named the root cause, it is still necessary to understand the nature of that problem. Without understanding the nature problem, you will not know what to expect when the problem in absent. Chapter 4, "Discerning Variation: Fluctuation in Processes and Outcomes," introduces you to the next principle in improvement science: focus on variation. By understanding variation in processes and outcomes, we locate the source of the problem—be it a flaw in the system or a more localized special event or phenomenon. Locating the source of the problem begins to tell us how to address it.

Key Terms

- **Deficit ideology**—Deficit ideology also known as deficit perspectives and deficit cognitive frames, is a world view that rationalizes and justifies inequitable outcomes as the result of deficiencies within individuals or their communities instead of broader systems. It is a form of "blaming the victim" that is rooted in hegemonic/dominant beliefs about superiority and inferiority. While deficit ideology was once rooted in eugenics and belief in genetic inferiority, it has morphed to beliefs in cultural inferiority. Deficit ideology would espouse a statement such as: poor people are poor because they are lazy.

- **Diversity Scorecard**—A Diversity Scorecard is a tool to help educators, in higher education primarily, view inequities within their organizations. Bensimon (2004) describes the tool as having three purposes—to prompt awareness, to interpret, and to act to resolve inequities in a collegiate setting.

- **Empathy interviews**—Empathy interviews are a qualitative data collection technique that helps practitioners understand the perspective of different stakeholders. They can be used during problem definition, as a part of seeing the system, or as a method to document implementation within the PDSA cycle. While advanced by design schools, empathy interviews are similar to qualitative interviewing techniques, especially ethnographic and phenomenological approaches to research.

- **Equity audit**—Equity audits are guides to examining data to determine where inequities may persist. Proportional representation is often a barometer for determining the extent of disproportionality or inequity in a particular domain.

- **Fishbone/Ishikawa diagram**—The fishbone diagram is a tool for delineating root causes of a particular problem of practice.

- **Five Whys technique**—The Five Whys technique is a root cause analysis process that helps practitioners get to the source of a problem by asking why—five times.

- **Inclusive Excellence Scorecard**—An Inclusive Excellence Scorecard is a tool to help educators, primarily in higher education, view inequities within their organizations. The IE Scorecard has four areas for assessment: access and equity, campus climate, diversity in formal and informal curricula, and learning and development.

- **Root cause analysis (RCA)**—Root cause analysis is a process for determining the underlying source for a problem. Root cause analysis is necessary when practitioners believe undesired outcomes are merely a symptom of a fundamental problem. There are many different approaches to root cause analysis.

- **User-centered**—To be user-centered, or user-centric, is to seek to understand problems of practice and solutions from the perspectives of those closest to the problem.
- **Solutionitis**—Solutionitis is the propensity of educators to jump to solutions before fully defining (understanding) the problem.

Questions for Improving with Equity in Mind: Who Is Involved? Who Is Impacted?

- Whose voices have we included as we defined our problem of practice?
- Whose voices have we left out of our problem-definition activities?
- Will addressing this problem of practice lead to greater opportunities to learn for *all* students?
- Will it lead to greater opportunities to learn for traditionally marginalized or underserved students?
- Are our identified root causes based on deficit understandings of the populations we serve?

References

Bensimon, E. M. (2004). The diversity scorecard: A learning approach to institutional change. *Change: The Magazine of Higher Learning, 36*(1), 44–52.

Bensimon, E. M. (2005). Closing the achievement gap in higher education: An organizational learning perspective. *New Directions for Higher Education, 2005*(131), 99–111.

Berwick, D. M. (2008). The science of improvement. *JAMA, 299*(10), 1182–1184.

Biag, M. (2019) Navigating the improvement journey with an equity compass. In R. Crow, B. Hinnant-Crawford, & D. Spaulding (Eds.), The *educational leader's guide to improvement science: Data, designs, and cases for reflection* (pp. 91–123). Gorham, Maine: Myers Education Press.

Bryk, A. S., Gomez, L. M., Grunow, A., & LeMahieu, P. G. (2015). *Learning to improve: How America's schools can get better at getting better.* Cambridge, MA: Harvard Education Press.

Card, A. J. (2017). The problem with '5 whys.' *BMJ Quality & Safety*, *26*(8), 671–677.

D'amico, D., Pawlewicz, R. J., Earley, P. M., & McGeehan, A. P. (2017). Where are all the Black teachers? Discrimination in the teacher labor market. *Harvard Educational Review*, *87*(1), 26–49.

Ford, D. Y. (1998). The underrepresentation of minority students in gifted education: Problems and promises in recruitment and retention. *The Journal of Special Education*, *32*(1), 4–14.

Frattura, E. M., & Capper, C. A. (2007). *Leading for social justice: Transforming schools for all learners*. Corwin Press.

Gorski, P. C. (2011). Unlearning deficit ideology and the scornful gaze: Thoughts on authenticating the class discourse in education. *Counterpoints*, *402*, 152–173.

Green, T. L. (2017). Community-based equity audits: A practical approach for educational leaders to support equitable community-school improvements. *Educational Administration Quarterly*, *53*(1), 3–39.

Groenke, S. L. (2010). Seeing, inquiring, witnessing: Using the equity audit in practitioner inquiry to rethink inequity in public schools. *English Education*, *43*(1), 83–96.

Harry, B., & Klingner, J. (2014). *Why are so many minority students in special education?* New York, NY: Teachers College Press.

Huelsman, M. (2015). The debt divide: The racial and class bias behind the" new normal" of student borrowing. New York, NY: Demos

Ishikawa, K. (1986). *Guide to quality control*. Tokyo, Japan: Asian Productivity Organization.

Kaplan, R. S., & Norton, D. P. (1992 reprinted in 2005). The balanced scorecard: measures that drive performance. *Harvard business review*, *83*(7), 172.

Ladson-Billings, G. (2007). Pushing past the achievement gap: An essay on the language of deficit. *The Journal of Negro Education*, 316–323.

Lankford, H., Loeb, S., & Wyckoff, J. (2002). Teacher sorting and the plight of urban schools: A descriptive analysis. *Educational evaluation and policy analysis*, *24*(1), 37–62.

Morgan, D. L. (1996). Focus groups. *Annual Review of Sociology*, *22*(1), 129–152.

Newmann, F. M., King, M. B., & Youngs, P. (2000). Professional development that addresses school capacity: Lessons from urban elementary schools. *American Journal of Education, 108*(4), 259-299.

Oakes, J. (1986). Tracking, inequality, and the rhetoric of reform: Why schools don't change. *Journal of Education, 168*(1), 60-80.

Rubin, H. J., & Rubin, I. S. (2005). *Qualitative interviewing: The art of hearing data* (2nd ed.). Thousand Oaks, CA: Sage.

Rush, C. B. and Robinson, G. (2019). Responding to teachers' perceptions: Addressing bias in the special education referral process. In B. Hinnant-Crawford, S. Platt, C. Newman, & A. Hilton (Eds.), *Comprehensive multicultural education in the 21st century: Increasing access in the age of retrenchment* (pp. 125-142). Charlotte, NC: Information Age Publishing.

Sensoy, O., & DiAngelo, R. (2017). *Is everyone really equal?: An introduction to key concepts in social justice education.* New York, NY: Teachers College Press.

Serrat, O. (2017). *Knowledge solutions.* Singapore: Springer.

Skrla, L., Scheurich, J. J., Garcia, J., & Nolly, G. (2004). Equity audits: A practical leadership tool for developing equitable and excellent schools. *Educational Administration Quarterly, 40*(1), 133-161.

Watanabe, K. (2009). *Problem solving 101: A simple book for smart people.* London: Penguin.

Williams, D. A., Berger, J. B., & McClendon, S. A. (2005). *Toward a model of inclusive excellence and change in postsecondary institutions.* Washington, DC: Association of American Colleges and Universities.

CHAPTER FOUR

Discerning Variation
Fluctuation in Processes and Outcomes

In the previous chapter, I argued it is critical to figure out the root cause of a problem instead of simply treating the symptom. Unfortunately, we often address symptoms first, and never get to the real problem. To determine the root cause, we will put principle 1 into praxis; we must be user-centered and problem specific. The first principle of improvement science is all about naming and identifying the root causes of problems of practice. The second principle of improvement science is also about understanding the problem of practice. In this chapter, we will go deeper into the question: *What is the exact problem I am trying to solve?* by asking *What can patterns in our symptoms tell us about our problems?* In this chapter, we will explore the improvement science principle 2: focus on variation. As we focus on variation, we will define different types of variation, review tools for monitoring variation, and illustrate how knowing your "normal" (or baseline) is a prerequisite for improvement in complex organizations.

What is Variation?

If you pick up some of the foundational improvement science or quality improvement texts that speak about the necessity for understanding statistical theory and variation, your eyes may glaze over. You may think back to an inferential statistics class and assumptions for a statistical test like the homogeneity of variance. "Is that the variance she's talking about?" you may be wondering. Variation is a natural part of life. If you look in a makeup case, you may see 12 tubes of lipstick, all some variation of red. And a stylist would tell you the wrong shade may not work with your outfit—even though technically they are all some shade of red. Variation matters! If we weigh ourselves several times during the day, we will find our weight fluctuates throughout the day; this is another example of variation. If the scale says you weigh .5lbs more after dinner than after breakfast, does that mean you have gained a half pound and should spend the next day fasting? Of course not, some variation is natural and to be expected.

As we try to understand the complex systems in which we work, we have to understand that some variation is to be expected and is not cause for alarm, while other instances of variation may indicate problems that need to be addressed. When thinking about organizational improvement, there are two types of variation you must consider and monitor (LeMahieu, Grunow, Baker, Nordstrum & Gomez, 2017). *Process variation* is variation in the implementation of desired tasks or performances. Many innovations fail not because of flawed logic, but because of flawed or *variable* implementation. When implementing a new intervention, we need to know the degree to which it was implemented as intended, or the degree to which implementation deviated from the initial plan.

For example, Course-Based Undergraduate Research Experiences, also known as CUREs, are an embedded deeper-learning pedagogy, designed to give larger numbers of undergraduate students opportunities to participate in authentic research experiences. Undergraduate research is considered a high impact practice. CUREs have also been argued to have the potential to increase opportunities for underrepresented populations to participate in undergraduate research, particularly women and people of color (Bangera & Brownell, 2014). If Professor Jones at Prestige State University decides to implement a CURE in his Biology 101 course, but he chooses the section designated for honors college students, can we assume the innovation worked as intended? Students in the Honors College may be better prepared for college, and that is often tied to secondary schools and community resources, which systematically favor students from wealthier families (who are less likely to be students of color). If Professor Jones's CURE does not increase the number of students of color considering STEM majors, was it because CUREs do not work, or because of the section selected to implement the CURE?

The second type of variation we must consider is outcome variation. *Outcome variation* is variation in desired outcomes, of which we are often more keenly aware (due to the fact that we measure outcomes more than we measure processes). Outcome variation is cause for concern when that variation produces undesirable outcomes (i.e., not performing at grade-level, or not returning for sophomore year of college), but it is increasingly damning when that variation can be predicted by immutable characteristics such as race or first-generation status.

Awareness of process and outcome variation are critical to ensuring equitable opportunities in educational systems. To be clear, this is not an endorsement of "gap-gazing," the type of research and data collection that simply collects and reports on disparities in achievement (Gutiérrez, 2008). Scholars acknowledge this type of inquiry can often be more harmful than useful and can reify deficit understandings of lower performing groups. Instead, improvement science suggests you should begin with knowing your baseline and your "normal." If you determine your normal is problematic, then you can do something about it.

Tools for Examining Variation

When you know the normal outputs of your system, you can identify when it may be appropriate to intervene to improve outcomes, and what type of intervention is appropriate. There are two categories of causes that influence your outcomes: special causes and common causes. Deming estimates that 6% of "troubles and possibilities for improvement" are due to special causes and 94% are due to common causes (or system issues). A *special cause* is a change in the variation (outcome) due to a specific local cause. A *common cause* is a fault within the system. If you are the principal of a school and your attendance falls to 60% for nearly two weeks, and you know there is an outbreak of flu or strep throat, there is no cause for alarm, even though your attendance has fallen below its normal 87%. The outbreak would be a "special cause." This is not to say that this special cause is not something you should work toward avoiding in the future nor that you won't have to work to try to mitigate the impact of all the instructional time lost because of the outbreak. You may encourage students to get vaccinated next year, or else hold Saturday academies to make up for lost instruction.

How, then, do you identify a special cause vs. a common cause? It is important to track the variation in your system so you are aware whether it is in a state of statistical control. What is statistical control? Statistical control is defined as "a stable process, one with no indication of a special cause of variation" (Deming, 2000, p. 321). To identify both special causes and a state of statistical control, you must be able to read charts that track variation. One such chart is the run chart.

Run Chart

A *run chart* is a simple but powerful tool that can help you understand the variation of processes and outcomes. And for my statisticians, while it appears to be descriptive in nature, it has properties that can help you make inferences about what to do next. A run chart plots measures over time, with the median as a reference line. When examining run charts, you look for trends, runs, and shifts (Perla, Provost & Murray, 2011).

Suppose you work in a Student Ethics office at Highly Prestigious University. You monitor the number of student infractions you receive weekly, by frequency and type. And you create a run chart for each type of infraction. Below are your infractions for cheating/plagiarism.

Figure 4.1. Run Chart Illustrating Number of Cheating/Plagiarism Infractions

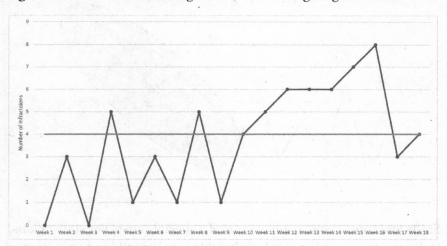

A *run* is series of points clustered on one side of the median before the line crosses the median. There are seven runs in this chart.

Figure 4.2. Run Chart with Runs Identified

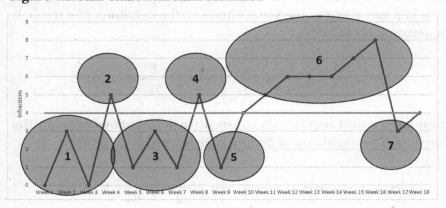

Weeks 11 through 15 (enclosed in circle 6) are indicative of a *shift*. A shift is signified by six or more consecutive points all above or below the median. Similar to a shift, a *trend* is five or more consecutive points going in the same direction.

Figure 4.3. Run Chart with Trend Identified

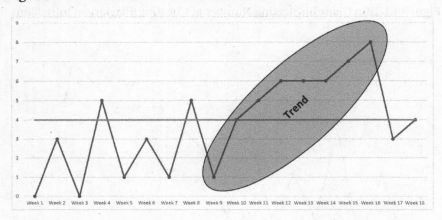

Shifts and trends can be indications of a special cause. For statisticians, shifts and trends indicate the probability that something in a system is unstable. And it is unlikely such a pattern will persist due to chance. When thinking about shifts and trends, remember, there is a 50/50 chance that each measure will fall either above or below the median or travel in the same direction as the previous point. The likelihood of five in a row going in the same direction, the definition of a trend, is approximately 3/100:

$$\frac{1}{2} * \frac{1}{2} * \frac{1}{2} * \frac{1}{2} * \frac{1}{2} = \frac{1}{32} = .03125$$

Similarly, a shift requires six consecutive points above or below the median. The likelihood of finding such a trend is < 2/100:

$$\frac{1}{2} * \frac{1}{2} * \frac{1}{2} * \frac{1}{2} * \frac{1}{2} * \frac{1}{2} = \frac{1}{64} = .01562$$

So, you are examining these ethics violations and trying to understand what this shift and trend at the latter part of the semester is trying to tell you. Your initial thought may be, "It's the end of semester crunch" and students are plagiarizing out of desperation. But when you examine further, and look at historical data you may find that it does not normally jump in this manner, and your mean has increased this semester. This is further indication of a special cause. Then you may investigate where these cases are originating. In your investigation, you find that 60% are coming from a new faculty member in the English department, who started this semester. She is using SafeAssign software to determine what percentage of a student's paper comes from other works and is submitting students for conduct violations if more than 20% comes up.

This is where you can intervene to address the special cause. You can ask her to add copyright and plagiarism objectives to her class, to ensure students are not accidentally plagiarizing, and that they have a clear understanding of her expectations.

Sometimes stable systems produce inequitable outcomes. If you are the Director of Special Education for Alliance Unified School District and you notice English Language Learners are disproportionately sent for evaluation year after year, the outcome is stable but the stable disproportionality is an indication of a flaw in the system. You may need to examine the referral process and where the referrals are originating. Some of your teachers may be confusing the need for language acquisition support with the need for intensive academic support. Likewise, if you notice African Americans make up 20% of your district and Latinx students make up 15% of your district, but their Advanced Placement enrollment has hovered around 5% and 7% of AP enrollment, respectively, for the last seven years, you have a stable, but problematic, system. And you need to ask why students from African American and Latinx students are not enrolling in (or being referred to) advanced placement courses.

Pareto Chart

The run chart is not the only tool you can use to help you understand outcome and process variation. Juran, another giant in quality improvement in production and manufacturing, was a proponent of using Pareto charts and understanding Pareto's Principle. Pareto was a French philosopher who spoke about the vital few verses the useful many; there are often multiple explanations or causes for some outcome, but usually some have more impact than others (Juran, 1989). As we are limited in time and resources, it is essential to turn your attention to the vital few instead of the useful many. Pareto's Principle suggests "80 percent of the variability in some outcomes is found to be associated with 20 percent of the possible causes" (Bryk et al., 2015, p. 176).

Imagine you are the principal at a large high school, with 4,500 students, and you have become increasingly interested in how discipline impacts opportunities to learn. You have examined your out of school suspension (OSS) data, and you were pleasantly surprised about the consistency across your administrative team with doling out OSS as a punishment. Across the board, your high school only gives OSS when the punishment for the behavior, as outlined in the code of conduct, requires suspension—primarily physical fights, bringing a weapon on campus, or drugs on campus. Your OSS rate has decreased dramatically since you initiated a schoolwide training, after the second 9 weeks, on how suspending children impacts their opportunity to learn.

Figure 4.4. Run Chart of OSS Data Before & After Intervention

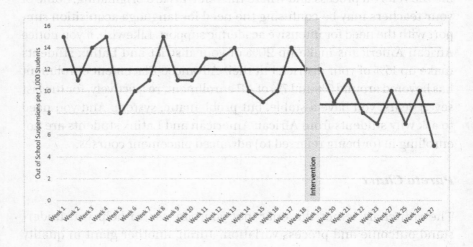

However, after examining your OSS data, you begin investigating your in-school suspension (ISS) data. At the same time your OSS decreased, your ISS increased. This may be an unintended consequence of your intervention to reduce OSS suspensions.

Figure 4.5. Run Chart of ISS Data Before & After Intervention

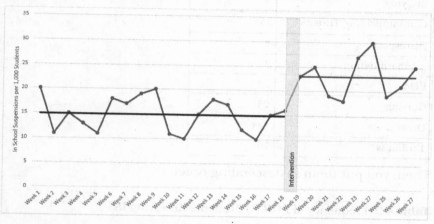

However, because ISS is a room with a monitor, not a teacher, and students are doing bookwork and are missing out on the rich pedagogy, discussion, and interaction of the classroom, your high ISS rates are still detrimental to your students' opportunity to learn. Your investigation leads you to study the reasons for ISS within the last 9 weeks. Within the last 9 weeks, you had a little over 900 in-school suspensions (approximately 100 each week) for a variety of explanations: bullying, communicating threats, disrespect, insubordination, public displays of affection, cursing/swearing, dress code violations, and tardiness. Because of your focus on equity, you disaggregate the data by varying student groups to see if some are being punished for certain violations more than others. You create multiple Pareto charts to help you understand variation in this outcome—one examining LGBTQ students and one examining African American students. African Americans make up 30% of your school but were 50% of the ISS cases. Similarly, LGBTQ students make up 15% of your school but were 30% of your ISS cases. Because of their overrepresentation, you wanted to look at them separately.

To create a Pareto chart, you begin with the number of ISS incidences by reason, in this case the explanations that lead to LGBTQ students receiving ISS.

Table 4.1. Frequency of LGBTQ Students Receiving ISS by Reason

Bullying	3
Communicating Threats	15
Disrespect	8
Insubordination	7
PDA	78
Cursing	25
Dress Code	124
Tardiness	10

Then, you put them in descending order.

Table 4.2. Frequency of LGBTQ Students Receiving ISS by Reason in Descending Order

Reason	Incidences
Dress Code	124
PDA	78
Cursing	25
Communicating Threats	15
Tardiness	10
Disrespect	8
Insubordination	7
Bullying	3
Total ISS for LGBTQ	270

Next, you calculate what percentage of the total each explanation represents. In this case, it will be calculated as the number of incidents in each category divided by the total number of incidents (270).

Table 4.3. Frequency of LGBTQ Students Receiving ISS Percent by Reason

Reason	Incidences	Percentage
Dress Code	124	45.93%
PDA	78	28.89%
Cursing	25	9.26%
Communicating Threats	15	5.56%
Tardy	10	3.70%
Disrespect	8	2.96%
Insubordination	7	2.59%
Bullying	3	1.11%

Lastly, you calculate the cumulative percentage (as a running total when you add each additional reason).

Table 4.4. Frequency of LGBTQ Students Receiving ISS Percent and Cumulative Percent by Reason

Reason	Incidences	Percentage	Cumulative Percentage
Dress Code	124	45.93%	45.93%
PDA	78	28.89%	74.82%
Cursing	25	9.26%	84.08%
Communicating Threats	15	5.56%	89.63%
Tardiness	10	3.70%	93.34%
Disrespect	8	2.96%	96.30%
Insubordination	7	2.59%	98.89%
Bullying	3	1.11%	100.00%

Once you have this information, you are ready to make your Pareto chart. A *Pareto chart* is a bar chart superimposed with a line graph. Together they show the distribution or frequency of some item of interest and the cumulative percentage of the total. The Pareto chart helps illuminate the vital few and helps you to distinguish the vital few from the useful many. As you see in Chart 6.6, the various infractions are on the x-axis of this chart. The number of infractions by LGBTQ students in on the left vertical axis, and the cumulative percentage on the right vertical axis.

Figure 4.6. Pareto Chart of LGBTQ Reasons for ISS

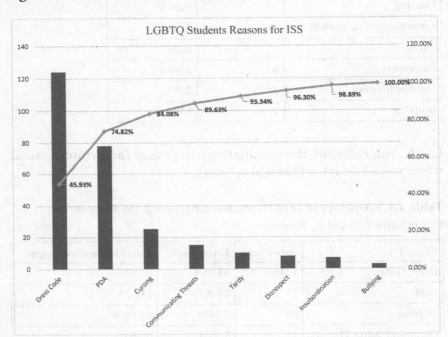

Research on LGBTQ students and discipline shows disproportionality in the enforcement of dress code and policy on public displays of affection (Hinnant-Crawford, Platt & Wingard, 2019; Snapp, Hoenig, Fields & Russell, 2014). In terms of fairness, you want to make sure rules against PDA are enforced across the board and that the policy is not being used to discriminate against non-heterosexual couples. Furthermore, you may want to think about how communication at home about ISS for PDA could have the potential to out a student. You also may be led to assess faculty perceptions, and determine the degree to which it is necessary to surveil and police this minoritized population.

You repeat the same exploration on your African American students. In this instance, you find that disrespect and insubordination are your most common reasons for ISS. This aligns with the literature that says African American students are more likely to experience exclusionary discipline for subjective reasons (Hinnant-Crawford et al., 2019; Skiba, Michael, Nardo & Peterson, 2002; Stone & Stone, 2011).

Figure 4.7. Pareto Chart of African American Students' Reasons for ISS

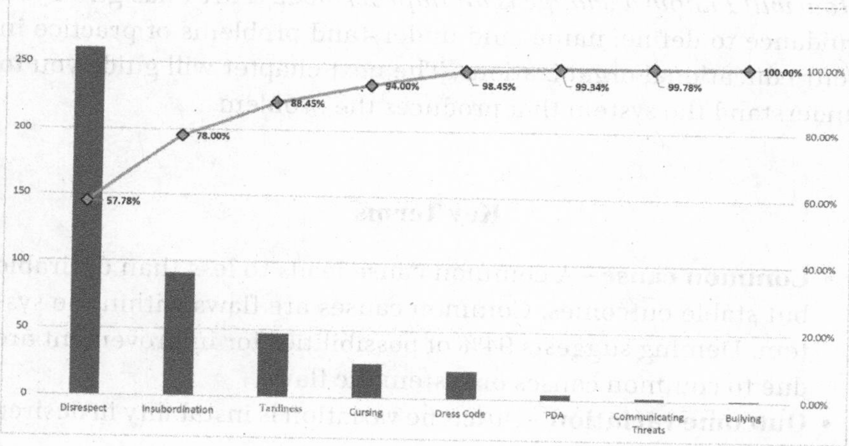

Scrutinizing the Pareto chart of your Black students could lead you to one of two conclusions: Black students are more disrespectful, or teachers interpret Black student behavior as disrespectful more often. This may lead you to a more in-depth analysis, examining the description of the behaviors or even following up with the teachers to see what they classify as disrespect or insubordination.

The run chart and the Pareto chart are two tools to help you closely examine what is happening in your organization. Disaggregating data using these charts can illuminate issues you may have otherwise missed. When Bryk and associates name "Focus on Variation in Performance" as one of the principles of improvement science, they are reminding you how important it is to *know your normal*. You do not want to misattribute special causes to common causes and vice versa. Only through analysis of your own data do you begin to uncover what is happening within your system. Your data will lead you to questions that will lead you to improvement.

The first two principles: *be user-centered and problem specific* and *focus on variation* are essential in defining and understanding the nature of our problems. The remaining four principles guide our thinking about how to address the problems to bring about real and expedient improvement. In section III of the primer, we take up the questions: *What change might I introduce and why?* and *How will I know a change is an improvement?* Part I has given you guidance to define, name, and understand problems of practice in your educational organizations. The next chapter will guide you to understand the system that produces the problem.

Key Terms

- **Common cause**—A common cause leads to less than desirable but stable outcomes. Common causes are flaws within the system. Deming suggests 94% of possibilities for improvement are due to common causes or systematic flaws.
- **Outcome variation**—Outcome variation is instability in desired outcomes.
- **Pareto chart**—A pareto chart is useful when examining sources or causes for variation (particularly errors). It is a bar chart with a line graph superimposed. The bar represents counts of particular causes or errors, and the line graph illustrates the cumulative percentage of the whole each bar represents. The Pareto Principle says 80% of variation is due to 20% of the causes; a Pareto chart helps you determine if this is the case, and can help you prioritize what issues to address first.
- **Process variation**—Process variation deals with change or fluidity in an organizational process or in the implementation of some intervention. Sometimes the goal of an improvement is to minimize process variation.
- **Run**—A run is a series of points on a run chart clustered on one side of the median.
- **Run chart**—A run chart is a line graph plots data on outcomes or processes over time (daily, weekly, etc.). A run chart also illustrates a median line for reference to determine when there are runs, shifts, and trends.

- **Shift**—A shift is when there are six or more consecutive points on the same side of the median.
- **Special cause**—A special cause is change in variation due to a specific localized cause.
- **Trend**—A trend is five or more points on a run chart moving in the same direction.

Questions for Improving with Equity in Mind: Who Is Involved? Who Is Impacted?

- When our outcomes are stable, does the data indicate we are producing similar outcomes across student groups?
  - Programs? Departments?
  - Colleges?
- Can variation in our outcomes be predicted by immutable or social characteristics possessed by our students?
- How are we tracking variation in our processes?
  - Do processes change based on who we are serving?

References

Bangera, G., & Brownell, S. E. (2014). Course-based undergraduate research experiences can make scientific research more inclusive. *CBE—Life Sciences Education, 13*(4), 602–606.

Gutiérrez, R. (2008). A "gap-gazing" fetish in mathematics education? Problematizing research on the achievement gap. *Journal for Research in Mathematics Education,* 357–364.

Hinnant-Crawford, B., Platt, C. S.. & Wingard, D. (2019). Law and disorder: Classroom management, discipline, and the promise of multicultural education. In B. Hinnant-Crawford, C. S. Platt, C. Newman, & A. Hilton (Eds.), *Comprehensive multicultural education in the 21st century: Increasing access in the age of retrenchment* (pp. 217–238). Charlotte, NC: Information Age Publishing.

Juran, J. M. (1989). *Juran on leadership for quality: An executive handbook.* New York, NY: The Free Press.

LeMahieu, P. G., Grunow, A., Baker, L., Nordstrum, L. E., & Gomez, L. M. (2017). Networked improvement communities: The discipline of improvement science meets the power of networks. *Quality Assurance in Education, 25*(1), 5–25.

Perla, R. J., Provost, L. P., & Murray, S. K. (2011). The run chart: A simple analytical tool for learning from variation in healthcare processes. *BMJ Quality & Safety, 20*(1), 46–51.

Skiba, R. J., Michael, R. S., Nardo, A. C., & Peterson, R. L. (2002). The color of discipline: Sources of racial and gender disproportionality in school punishment. *The Urban Review, 34*(4), 317–342.

Snapp, S. D., Hoenig, J. M., Fields, A., & Russell, S. T. (2014). Messy, butch, and queer: LGBTQ youth and the school-to-prison pipeline. *Journal of Adolescent Research, 30*(1), 57–82. doi:10.1177/0743558414557625

Stone, D. H., & Stone, L. S. (2011). Dangerous & disruptive or simply cutting class; When should schools kick kids to the curb: An empirical study of school suspension and due process rights. *Journal of Law & Family Studies, 13*(1), 1–42.

SECTION THREE

What Change Might
I Introduce and Why?
How Will I Know the Change
Is an Improvement?

In 2012, the American Educational Research Association's theme for their annual meeting was: *Non Satis Scire*—to know is not enough. After you have defined your problem and you know its root cause, or you know the normal variation in outcomes and processes in your organization, that is not enough to improve. Knowing is essential, but knowledge of the problem alone will not improve it.

The succeeding section of this text deals with the latter two essential questions:

- How do I know a change is an improvement?
- What change might I introduce, and why?

As stated in the previous section, the order of the essential questions is inconsequential, but normally, ***How will I know a change is an improvement?*** is depicted before ***What change might I introduce and why?*** The first question operationalizes what it means to improve. Answering the second question, what change you might introduce and why, means you understand what might work in your context. That is the question we will take up first in chapter 5.

The principles that guide these chapters do not map onto the essential questions in a one-to-one manner. These questions bleed through several principles. Seeing the system is vital for determining what changes could work in your context. However, developing a theory of improvement is both a part of seeing the system and developing practical measurements. Practical measurement operationalizes your theory and helps you uncover if a change is really an improvement. In the next three chapters, we will uncover tools and strategies to help you answer both those questions during the improvement process.

In Part III of the primer, we get to the heart of improvement science, the Plan-Do-Study-Act method. Its iterative nature reminds me of Ella Baker and her declaration that, "We who believe in freedom cannot rest until it comes." Improvement is not a "one shot and you are finished." Addressing wicked problems in complex systems requires an iterative approach and relentless persistence toward the goal.

The final chapter deals with accelerating improvement through the use of networks. Networking and sharing ideas prioritize collaboration over competition. This section challenges you to approach problems of practice in unconventional ways, ways that would revolutionize our ability to improve.

CHAPTER FIVE

Using a Wide-Angle Lens
Seeing the System Producing Your Outcomes

Thanks to the advent of the smartphone and DLSR cameras, everyone is a photographer now. You can zoom in and zoom out and move around to capture the perfect photo. Those who used to shoot with Canons and Nikons less than 20 years ago and those who take photos professionally know the importance of selecting the correct lens to capture the shot. A telephoto lens can give the illusion of subjects far away being close, and can let you blur out some unnecessary detail, so only your subject is in focus. On the other hand, a wide-angle lens can give you a wide view of a scene, with lots of details. When it comes to understanding problems of practice, a telephoto lens alone will not allow you to see the necessary information to make decisions about how to improve. A wide-angle lens is a necessity—because you need to see with clarity the entire system that produces the results. Individuals are like telephoto lenses, but collaboration can lead you to a wide-angle view of your system.

Your perspective through your telephoto lens has allowed you to see the symptoms of the problem. By being user-centered and problem specific and by paying attention to variation (principles 1 and 2) you may have identified some root causes and determined if the cause was a common cause or special cause. Your attention to variation has led you to understand your system's normal outputs. In this chapter, I will advise you to zoom out, so you can see and understand the system that produces your problem of practice. The third principle of improvement science is to *see the system producing the results.* More specifically, this chapter acknowledges the complexity of educational institutions and the difficulty of determining cause and effect (problem and solution) in complex organizations. As you address problems of practice in your organization, you must continuously ask yourself: *How is our organization (policies, procedures, practices, priorities, personnel) contributing to the problem of practice (intentionally or unintentionally)?*

In this chapter, I will introduce you to a number of tools to help scaffold your ability to view your organization with a wide-angle lens. We will explore the nature of complexity, systems thinking, and how failure to consider your system's complexity will lead to great ideas for change that will have unintended consequences. This chapter also explores some of our most vexing educational problems, such as the opportunity gap, as the result of intersecting complex systems.

Educational Systems

Every system is perfectly designed to get the results it gets.
—Central Law of Improvement

*I view inequality in educational outcomes as a learning problem
of institutional actors—faculty members, administrators,
counselors, and others—rather than as a learning problem of
students, the more typical interpretation.*
—Estela Maria Bensimon (2005, p. 100)

When Horace Mann took great steps to start the common school movement, he envisioned an organizational structure that would provide all citizens with the basic skills and knowledge to be able to participate in the democracy. Hochschild and Scovronick (2010) talk about the dual functions of public education—to educate a citizen, but also to train in personal functions, such as to be able to sustain oneself, also to help with self-actualization and the realization of one's own potential. What we have, though, is the system John Dewey prophesied about in the early 20th century, where you have a system that educates some into masters and others into slaves. Despite Horace Mann's intent when the common schools were created, they were not created for everyone. The history of exclusion of certain groups in education has been well-documented elsewhere (Ladson-Billings, 2006). But as we have tried to integrate others into a system that was not created for them, we have witnessed differential outcomes among these different groups.

The central law of improvement is that every system is perfectly designed to get the results it gets (Langley et al., 2009). What is that telling you? It is saying the school system in the United States of America is designed for impoverished children to underachieve, for children of color to be overrepresented in special education and underrepresented in gifted education, for children of color and LGBTQ students to be disproportionately disciplined and excluded. As you ask questions about what works, for whom, and under what circumstances, in the case of education, you may see the system works best for those for whom it was designed.

We often identify students from traditionally minoritized or underserved communities as at-risk. If a student has been retained in elementary grades, they are considered at-risk for dropping out. If a student at the community college is placed into remedial courses, they are described as at-risk for never getting into a curricular (associates degree) program. If a student is a conditional admit at the university, they are designated at-risk during their probationary period. Edmund Gordon (1999) explains that the conception of at-risk is a misnomer, and at-risk is not an adjective of the student, but tells you more about the environment. Gordon articulates, "Being at-risk of failure may be an iatrogenic condition; that is, it may be more appropriately conceptualized as a condition of circumstance brought on by the failure or incapacity of the developmental environment to support the needs of the developing person" (1999, p. 35). Individuals are not at-risk; environments are risk inducing. You take the same at-risk student and put them in some alternative environment, they may excel whereas *you* may feel at-risk. How are systems that are conducive to the education of some risk inducing to the education of others?

The current educational system is perfectly designed for the results it produces. What does that mean? What does that mean for educators who desire to close gaps in opportunities, and help all students realize their full potential? It means when looking for changes or solutions, one cannot be narrowly focused but should look at the entire system that creates these results. And that requires systems thinking.

Systems Thinking

Part of Deming's Profound Knowledge was an appreciation for systems. But what exactly is systems thinking? In his well-known book, *The Fifth Discipline: The Art and Practice of Learning Organizations*, Peter Senge defines *systems thinking* as, "a discipline for seeing the 'structures' that underlie complex situations, and for discerning high from low leverage change" (2006, p. 69). Senge goes on to say that systems thinking is about training our minds to see the integrated whole instead of disconnected parts.

Recommended Addition for the Improvement Scientist's Bookshelf

As stated in the previous chapter, a *system* is made up of interconnected parts bound by some shared aim. Systems theory goes into greater detail than Deming's simplified definition about what makes a system. A system is more than the sum of its parts. This is often referred to as holism or *emergence*; the system becomes something greater than the sum of its parts. Eggs, sugar, flour, butter, milk, and heat are all things you can find in a kitchen. Each is useful on its own. But when combined correctly, cake emerges. Cake is something different from just the ingredients in a bowl. Sullivan (2011) explains that in complex systems, "emergence disguises cause and effect" (para. 2).

Systems can be described as complicated or complex. Complicated systems have different moving parts, but those parts "operate in patterned ways" (Sargut & McGrath, 2011, para. 7). Furthermore, in a complicated system, "one can usually predict outcomes by knowing the starting conditions. In a complex system, the same starting conditions can produce different outcomes, depending on the interactions of the elements in the system" (Sargut & McGrath, 2011, para. 8). A system's *complexity* is a function of the multiplicity (number) of components, the diversity or heterogeneity of its components, and their interdependence. The more they depend on each other, the greater the necessity for cooperation. The more diverse they are, sometimes the more difficult it becomes for each component to understand the function and needs of the other.

In universities, there are often two major systems operating simultaneously to support students: academic affairs and student affairs. Often, people on one side of the house (academic affairs) know very little about the other side of the house (student affairs). Yet, if a student is underperforming because she is housing-insecure and is concerned about the closing of school during spring break, it would probably take academic interventions to pull up her grades, as well as student affairs (housing, student support services, counseling, etc.) interventions to ensure her well-being. Two separate components that are heterogeneous, being run by different individuals with different priorities, that are both essential for the success of the university—this comprises a complex system.

This principle says we must *see the system that produces the results*, which requires systems thinking. Senge argues there are two major components of systems thinking—seeing interrelationships and seeing processes—where you are socialized to see cause and effects chains snapshots. This is a shift of mind and must be intentional. Our failure to see systems leads to deficit understandings about populations we serve. Much of the inequality we witness that we would like to attribute to personal responsibility is actually the outcome of complex sociopolitical realities.

Opportunity Gaps as the Outcome on Complex Systems

Linda Darling-Hammond and Rich Milner have both described gaps in educational opportunity as the result of complex systems. In her book, *The Flat Earth and Education*, Darling-Hammond has a chapter called "The Anatomy of Inequality: How Opportunity Gaps Are Constructed." She names five components that contribute to gaps in opportunities to learn: poverty and lack of social supports, limited early learning opportunities, re-segregation and unequal schooling, access (or lack there of) to qualified teachers, and access (or lack there of) to high quality curriculum. While each component is distinct, there are varying degrees of interconnectedness. For instance, limited early learning opportunities are going to be more prevalent when there are more impoverished communities. She argues that these things work in tandem to create a perfect storm of inequitable access to opportunities to learn. While this is not a Deming system, no one would argue there is an aim of inequitable access; one can argue that here the system is greater than the sum of the parts—emergence is real. Their impacts are not additive, where if you subtract one, you subtract this amount of inequality. She has, in fact, painted the picture of a societal system that produces educational inequality.

Rich Milner also examines the opportunity gap, but more on a micro level than on the macro level featured in Darling-Hammond's anatomy of inequality. Milner (2012) poses a critical question that systems thinkers should also ask, "Why do so many educational researchers focus on outcomes instead of the processes that lead to those outcomes?" (p. 696). His delineation of the factors contributing to the gaps illustrates the complex interplay between teacher/instructor perceptions and the classroom environment. According to Milner, a deficit mindset and low expectations, colorblindness, the myth of meritocracy, context-neutral mindsets, and cultural conflicts are all components of the system that influences opportunities to learn at an interpersonal or classroom level.

Darrius Stanley (2019) explains that equity work takes place on three levels: interpersonal (classroom), organizational (school/college), and structural (societal) level (D. Stanley, personal communication, 2019). To systematically address inequity, working on one level alone would be inadequate. Milner's system describes the classroom where deficit ideology and low expectations of teachers lead to lower academic achievement. On the college level, Suárez-Orozco and associates illustrate how micro-aggressions based on race, gender, and perceived intelligence are often a part of the student experience (where the perpetrators of these offenses are often faculty). On the institutional level, you have to ask, *What policies are in place that may create barriers for students? How inclusive is the campus climate?* On the structural level, *How does re-segregation impact the political will of certain constituencies to support public schools?* Educational inequality is so much more complex than the common narratives of incompetent educators or educators who do not care. To address inequality, it is necessary to first examine the system, or multiple systems, that interact to produce the results.

Figure 5.1. Complex Systems and Opportunity Gaps

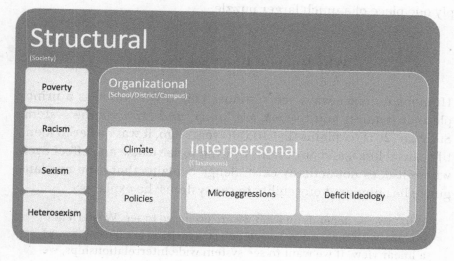

When you take a systems view, you realize why educators have to be careful not to make well-intentioned but erroneous comments such as "my intervention will alleviate the opportunity gap." Chances are it will not, but it may be a piece of the puzzle that dismantles this system. For practical and psychological reasons, it is critically important for you to see the system. Equity work is hard, and results are not always immediate.

1. Seeing the system helps you make better choices about who should be at the table to inform improvement work.
2. Seeing the system helps you make better selections of interventions to address problems of practice.
3. Seeing the system helps you understand that there are a myriad of influences on the outcome you seek. If you choose to work in one area and do not get the results you desire, you must realize you only addressed one part of a complex problem.

Number three is critically important for people involved in justice-oriented work. Equity is a long game; it is easy to feel tired, fatigued, or defeated when you look narrowly at your plan and it did not produce the desired outcome. Yet, when you are examining from a systems view, you can begin to understand your plan is simply one piece of a much larger puzzle.

Why Humans Don't See Systems

Humans do not always see systems. This is why there is a principle that requires you to *look, see, study, and examine* the system. Sullivan (2011) explains that 10,000 years ago, it was easier to identify causal links, and our brains evolved to see cause and effect even where it does not actually exist. Senge explains that even our language has hindered our ability to see systems; he explains:

> What we see depends on what we are prepared to see. Western languages, with their subject-verb-object structure, are biased toward a linear view. If we want to see system wide interrelationships, we

need a language of interrelationships, a language made up of circles. Without such language, our habitual ways of seeing the world produce fragmented views and counterproductive actions . . . Such language is important in facing dynamically complex issues and strategic choices, especially when individuals, teams, and organizations need to see beyond events and into the forces that shape change. (Senge, 2006, pp. 73–74)

Similarly, Asante (1998) opines, this "inability to 'see' from several angles is perhaps the one common weakness in provincial scholarship" (p. 1). Sullivan goes on to describe human behaviors that contribute to our inability to see the system in complex organizations. First, we rely too much on the advice and suggestions of experts. While expertise has its place, expert predictions can be fallible. Second, according to Sullivan (2011), we are "reluctant to share private information, so we aggregate information poorly" (para. 13). This means even when the right stakeholders are at the table, they may be withholding information that is key to understanding the system, or predicting how some intervention will impact the system. To improve systems and the outcomes of systems, you have to first recognize the system that is producing the results.

When We Fail to See the System: Unintended Consequences

Today's problems come from yesterday's "solutions."
—Senge, 2006, p. 58

Our failure to see systems, intentionally or not, leads to unintended consequences. More than half a century ago, the *Brown* decision of 1954 changed the landscape of American education and public institutions writ large. The U.S. Supreme Court's ruling that "'separate but equal' has no place. Separate educational facilities are inherently unequal," had broad, sweeping implications across the country (*Brown vs. Board of Education*, 1954). Civil rights activists, organizations like the National Association for the Advancement of Colored People (NAACP), and Black educators who advocated for

Black access to White institutions were seeking to secure greater resources for their students—newer texts, lab facilities, etc. But this change had detrimental effects on the Black community. As a result of *Brown*, between 1954 and 1965, 38,000 Black educators were fired in 17 southern states (Tillman, 2004). *Brown* had decimating impacts on the Black middle class. Tillman explains, "The loss of income for a group that was already being paid less than their White counterparts proved to be devastating to the economy of the African American community. Teaching was one of the few vocations open to formally educated Blacks. Thus, the economic balance of the Black community . . . was disturbed" (p. 298). Furthermore, while it had been predicted by some (DuBois, 1935), the school environments in which Black students were integrated were not always the most welcoming, and covert segregation persisted through tracking, over identification in special education, and disciplinary exclusion. This change in one part of the system had unforeseen and unintentional consequences in other parts of the system. Could the architects of desegregation have anticipated the impact on the teaching force?

More recent history also demonstrates unintended outcomes of educational decisions. The accountability regime has laudable intent. The chapter on problem definition advises the disaggregation of data to make sure everyone is achieving. So, how is it that some scholars believe accountability has exacerbated gaps in achievement? In my own research, I suggest accountability is detrimental to instruction because scores are becoming valued more than learning (Hinnant-Crawford, 2019). Educational triage, focusing on bubble kids who can most likely pass the exam to the detriment of lower performing students (Booher-Jennings, 2005) and removing students from the testing pool (via retention or special education placement), is an unintended consequence of a high stakes accountability system that hurts the children the policies are designed to help (Heilig & Darling-Hammond, 2008; Jacob, 2005). Could well-intended educational reformers have anticipated some of these behaviors as a result of accountability? Can you anticipate the unintended consequences of your improvement initiative?

A critical component of being an improvement scientist is to see the system that produces the results. Langley et al. (2009) explain the central law of improvement is that every system is perfectly designed to get the results it gets. This is essential to our understanding of how to improve. You have to understand the system in which you are working. Also, when you see the outcomes as a result of the system, you are less likely to fall victim to deficit perspectives, blaming students and/or their communities for unwanted outcomes.

Tools for Exploring Systems

As stated earlier, systems thinking takes intentionality. Luckily, there are tools that can help you scaffold your ways of thinking and illuminate the systems in which you operate.

Systems Map

There are a number of visual tools that can be used to help you see the system that is producing the results. The first of these tools is the systems map. A *systems map* illustrates the components and boundaries of a system at a particular point in time. This means the map is temporal and will change over time. While there is guidance on creation of maps, there is no exact set of rules. Some people prefer the components of the system to be drawn with fluid lines or in non-geometric shapes. Fluid shapes are used to illustrate the components are not rigid so as not to give an illusion of precision. Some system maps illustrate the relationships between components, and some just illustrate the components involved. See the example below:

Figure 5.2 . Systems Map of EdD Program at Regional Comprehensive University

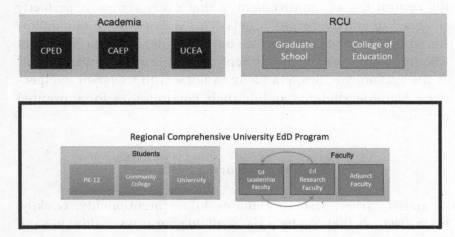

This is an extraordinarily simple system map of an academic program, an EdD program in Educational Leadership at Regional Comprehensive University. The primary components (or actors) in this system are faculty and students. The program is the system under examination in this example, not the college or the institution. Here the interdependence between leadership faculty and research faculty is illustrated with bidirectional arrows. When drafting a system map, you may begin drafting alone and then ask other individuals what is missing. Or you may begin in a group, using stakeholders from each of the major components of the system. Either way, you cannot end with just your view of the system; your myopic view will be incomplete. The image above neglects the support staff who are also key stakeholders in the EdD program.

In addition to the key components within the system, the map illustrates other environmental influences that may impact the system. In this case, the program is situated within a college of education. However, because it is a graduate program, it also has ties to the graduate school. The program is also a part of higher education in the United States. This particular program is a member of several consortia that speak about best practice in education: the Carnegie Project on the Education Doctorate (CPED), the University Council on Education Administration (UCEA), and Council for the Accreditation of Educator Preparation (CAEP). While these organizations are not a part of the system itself, they inform the system and the environment in which the system operates. This is why it may be useful to include them on the system map.

Sometimes, you want your map to communicate more than the components of the system. If that is the case, you are probably more apt to begin with a simple map showing the components, and then move into a more complex map that illustrates different challenges or opportunities for the system. A map is a map; what you know about traditional maps applies to system maps. You create a key and define that key. Below, the key uses different symbols for program, organization, and field challenges. You can choose what you want to include on the system map, but the components and the boundaries of the system must be there.

Figure 5.3. Systems Map of EdD Program Challenges at Regional Comprehensive University

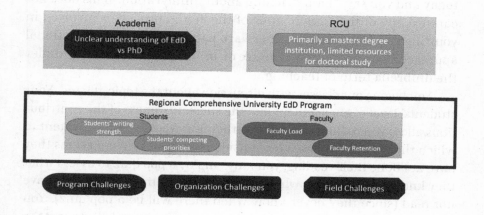

Systems Diagram

Because of the interdependence of different system components and the autonomous decision-making that impacts other components in the system, it is difficult to understand cause and effect in a complex system. Sullivan (2011) explains, "When you see something occur in a complex adaptive system, your mind is going to create a narrative to explain what happened—even though cause and effect are not comprehensible in that kind of system" (Sullivan, para. 11). A *systems diagram* is a tool that can help you train your mind to see circles of influence instead of linear cause and effect. In fact, Senge explains, "In systems thinking it is an axiom that every influence is both *cause* and *effect* [original emphasis]. Nothing is ever influenced in just one direction" (2006, p. 75).

Pretend you are an English instructor, and in an attempt to be multidisciplinary, you are using *The Book of the Unknown Americans* by Christina Henriquez as a literary text, historical and contemporary immigration policy documents, and nonfiction writing on the Iran-Contra affair to contextualize U.S. involvement in the destabilization of Central and South America. Your goal is to paint a big picture of the immigration crisis. You are really proud of this unit you have developed. Your supervisor asks what you are doing in class today and you say, "I am teaching about immigration." This does not capture any of the complexities of the actual processes involved in your instruction. However, there are patterns in your instructional approach that you may be unaware of, or that you may collapse under the umbrella term of teaching.

You begin your classes with discussion about the topic at hand. Your students' level of engagement and the substantiveness of the contributions allow you to informally assess their knowledge (and the extent to which they have completed the outside readings). When it seems they have not done their reading, you may employ a pop quiz to assess what they know, reward those who have read, and motivate those who have not read (since they never know when there will be a pop quiz). You complete the class with a mini lecture because you need all students to know the information, even those who have not done the reading.

A systems diagram would illustrate that as follows:

Figure 5.4 . Initial Systems Diagram

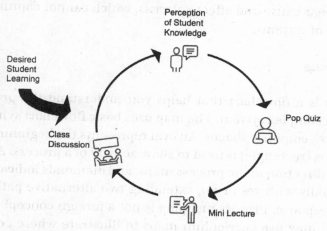

The behaviors employed are all driven by the desired learning you hope to cultivate in your students. But the discussion influences your perception of their knowledge, which in turn influences whether or not you decide to give a pop quiz. Because the classroom is complex and you are not the sole element, we can see interacting diagrams from the student perspective. Here, the pop quiz leads to uncertainty (and maybe even anxiety), possibly leading students to study more in order to be better prepared for the next class.

Figure 5.5. Interacting Systems Diagram

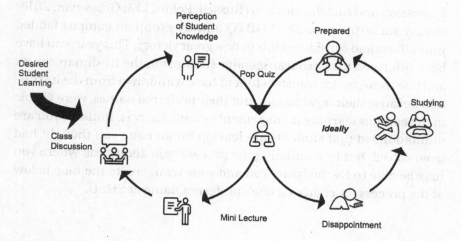

A systems diagram is one tool in an arsenal that tries to break us from seeing linear cause and effect patterns, which cannot capture the complexity of systems.

Process Mapping

A *process map* is a flowchart that helps you understand the processes within a complex system. The map uses basic flowchart symbols—which are geometric shapes. An oval represents the beginning or the end; a box (rectangle) is used to show activity of a process. An arrow denotes direction in the process maps, and diamonds indicate a decision, usually with yes or no, extending two alternative paths based on the response. Process mapping is not a foreign concept to educators. You may use curriculum maps to illustrate where certain material will be covered during the school year or what course covers certain standards in a course of study. The benefit of a process map is it allows you to focus on where the process may be failing, and thereby identify parts of the process to improve.

Imagine you are the Chief Diversity Officer at Southern Hospitality State University in the southern part of the United States. Last academic year, your team celebrated a victory of getting the university's database to display transgender students' preferred names. You presented the case: Research shows that using transgender students' preferred names and chosen pronouns is correlated with lower rates of depression and suicidal ideation (Russell, Pollitt, Li & Grossman, 2018) among such students. The LGBTQ affinity group on campus lauded your efforts and considered this to be a great victory. This year, you have been informed that two transgender students in the freshman cohort and one transgender transfer student have withdrawn from the institution because their legal names, not their preferred names, were visible in the campus learning management system, Canvas. Initially, you are dumbfounded that students are leaving for an issue you thought had been solved, but by examining the process, you determine where you may be able to fix the issue. You and your team create the map below of the process for changing one's preferred name at SHSU.

Figure 5.6. Initial Process Map for Preferred Name Change at SHSU

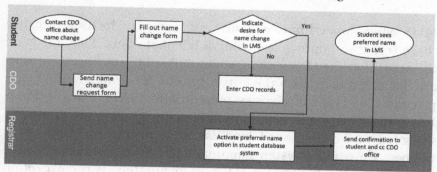

After an examination of the process, you noticed a failure in the system. All three of the students who left were unaware of how the process should start. Because of the celebrations on campus last year, returning students were aware of the first step, whereas incoming students (freshman and transfer) were not. You decided to alter the process yourself, instead of leaving it to the students. You will address incoming students at orientation and send a campus-wide email with the process for changing preferred names. Your revised process is shown in Figure 5.6:

Figure 5.7. Revised Process Map for Preferred Name Change at SHSU

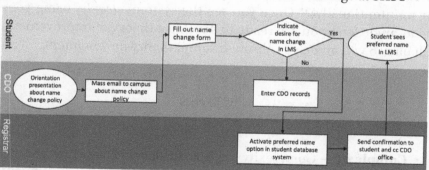

Process maps make explicit steps we often forget or overlook. In examining your process, you realize that initially the onus was on the student to initiate changes, and there was no mechanism for making students aware of that process.

Use a Wide-Angle Lens

Most educational improvements are narrowly focused because those trying to improve are using a telephoto lens. They focus on the areas that they know most about and fail to see how what they are doing interacts with the entire system. Most interventions are piecemeal and do not take a systematic approach. One exception is Integrated Comprehensive Systems for Equity (ICS for Equity™), designed and championed by Elise M. Frattura and Colleen A. Capper. They take a systems approach to bringing about equitable education in the K-12 arena. This, unfortunately, is the exception and not the rule. So, as you proceed in your improvement journey, remember the system. Using system maps, system diagrams, and process maps can help you to see the entire system producing the current outcomes. Take time to understand how your problem interacts with other parts of the system. Design your team based on people who have different points of views on the system, so that collectively, you can composite a complete picture. Failure to do so will result in unintended consequences. As a scholar-practitioner oriented toward justice, never forget to ask yourself and your team: "How is our organization (policies, procedures, practices, priorities, personnel) contributing to the problem of practice (intentionally or unintentionally)?" Once you see the system, *clearly*, using your wide-angle lens, you are ready to develop a theory of improvement. Chapter 6 will guide you through sound theory development.

Key Terms

- **Complexity**—Complexity is used to describe and understand systems. A system's complexity is a result of its multiplicity (number of parts), diversity or heterogeneity of those parts, and the degree of their interdependence.
- **Emergence**—Emergence is a concept that suggests the system is more than the sum of the separate parts within the system.

- **Opportunity gaps**—Opportunity gaps are not synonymous with achievement gaps; those gaps in achievement are symptoms of gaps in opportunity. The phrase "opportunity gap" is used to describe differential access to resources and educational opportunities experienced by different groups of students.
- **Process map**—A process map is a flowchart that illustrates the processes (and in some cases responsible parties) within a complex system.
- **System**—A system is an entity (organization) made of interconnected parts bound by a common purpose.
- **Systems diagram**—A systems diagram is a visual schematic to help illustrate circles of influence within systems, scaffolding systems thinkers away from linear understandings of cause and effect.
- **Systems map**—A systems map illustrates the components and boundaries of a system.
- **Systems thinking**—Systems thinking is an approach to viewing problems as the result of systems and helps to illuminate the variety of systems at play in complex situations.

Questions for Improving with Equity in Mind: Who Is Involved? Who Is Impacted?

- How is our organization (policies, procedures, practices, priorities, personnel) contributing to the problem of practice (intentionally or unintentionally)?
- What facets of our system (policies, procedures, processes, practices, culture, climate) are risk-inducing for certain populations?
  - Who are they risk-inducing for?
- Whose voices do we need at the table to have a clear understanding of the system producing our current outcomes?
- To what extent are our systems outcomes influenced by structural, organizational, and interpersonal factors?
  - Where do we have the most leverage to intervene?

References

Asante, M. K. (1998). *The Afrocentric idea*. Philadelphia, PA: Temple University Press.

Bensimon, E. M. (2005). Closing the achievement gap in higher education: An organizational learning perspective. *New Directions for Higher Education, 2005*(131), 99–111.

Booher-Jennings, J. (2005). Below the bubble: "Educational triage" and the Texas accountability system. *American Educational Research Journal, 42*(2), 231–268.

Darling-Hammond, L. (2015). *The flat world and education: How America's commitment to equity will determine our future*. New York, NY: Teachers College Press.

Du Bois, W. E. B. (1935). Does the Negro need separate schools? *Journal of Negro Education 4*(3), 423–431.

Gordon, E. W. (1999). *Education and justice: A view from the back of the bus*. New York, NY: Teachers College Press.

Gorski, P. C. (2011). Unlearning deficit ideology and the scornful gaze: Thoughts on authenticating the class discourse in education. *Counterpoints, 402*, 152–173.

Heilig, J. V., & Darling-Hammond, L. (2008). Accountability Texas-style: The progress and learning of urban minority students in a high-stakes testing context. *Educational Evaluation and Policy Analysis, 30*(2), 75–110.

Hinnant-Crawford, B. N. (2019). Legislating instruction in urban schools: Unintended consequences of accountability policy on teacher-reported classroom goal structures. *Urban Education*, 0042085919838004.

Hochschild, J. L., & Scovronick, N. (2003). *The American dream and the public schools*. Oxford, UK: Oxford University Press.

Jacob, B. A. (2005). Accountability, incentives, and behavior: The impact of high-stakes testing in Chicago public schools. *Journal of Public Economics, 89*, 761–796.

Ladson-Billings, G. (2006). From the achievement gap to the education debt: Understanding achievement in US schools. *Educational researcher, 35*(7), 3–12.

Langley, G. J., Moen, R. D., Nolan, K. M., Nolan, T. W., Norman, C. L., & Provost, L. P. (2009). *The improvement guide: A practical approach to enhancing organizational performance.* Hoboken, NJ: John Wiley & Sons.

Milner, H. R., IV. (2012). Beyond a test score: Explaining opportunity gaps in educational practice. *Journal of Black Studies, 43*(6), 693–718.

Russell, S. T., Pollitt, A. M., Li, G., & Grossman, A. H. (2018). Chosen name use is linked to reduced depressive symptoms, suicidal ideation, and suicidal behavior among transgender youth. *Journal of Adolescent Health, 63*(4), 503–505.

Sargut, G., & McGrath, R. G. (2011). Learning to live with complexity. *Harvard business review, 89*(9), 68–76.

Senge, P. M. (2006). *The fifth discipline: The art and practice of the learning organization.* New York, NY: Broadway Business.

Suárez-Orozco, C., Casanova, S., Martin, M., Katsiaficas, D., Cuellar, V., Smith, N. A., & Dias, S. I. (2015). Toxic rain in class: Classroom interpersonal microaggressions. *Educational Researcher, 44*(3), 151–160.

Sullivan, T. (2011). Embracing complexity. *Harvard Business Review*, 89(9), 89–92.

Tillman, L. C. (2004). (Un)intended consequences? The impact of the Brown v. Board of Education decision on the employment status of black educators. *Education and Urban Society, 36*(3), 280–303.

Warren, E. & Supreme Court of The United States. (1953) *U.S. Reports: Brown v. Board of Education, 347 U.S. 483.* [Periodical] Retrieved from the Library of Congress, https://www.loc.gov/item/usrep347483/.

CHAPTER SIX

Developing Theories
to Drive Improvement

The tools presented in the previous chapter help you to the see the system that is producing the results. Only once you have a good understanding of the system and the processes can you begin to develop and informed theory of improvement. You may be asking, *What does theory have to do with it?* If so, I would like to remind you of the epistemological underpinnings of improvement science, whereby knowledge is generated through the articulation, testing, and revising of theory. Yet, you cannot develop a sound theory of improvement without having a clearly defined problem and an understanding of the system that produces the current results.

Developing theory is not an improvement science principle; on the contrary, it is a practice that underlies the improvement science process. This chapter is devoted to the practice of developing theory, because it is so essential to successful improvement. In this chapter, I will define a theory of improvement (also known as a theory of practice improvement), tell you what leads to sound theory, and give you tools to help refine and communicate your theory to others within (or outside of) your organization. Embedded in developing theory is the process of developing changes or interventions to address the problem of practice. Finally, this chapter will also offer suggestions for developing and selecting changes to implement to address problems of practice.

Theory of Improvement

A theory of improvement answers the second essential improvement science question: *What change might I introduce to solve my problem of practice and why?* The root cause analysis, the run charts, the system and process maps are all tools to help you understand the problem you are facing and how the system creates and/or maintains that problem. You can create a theory of how to fix the problem without knowing these things, but that theory will probably be futile in the final analysis.

In education, there are all types of theories. There are longstanding, empirically supported theories, such as social cognitive theory, cultural historical activity theory, critical race theory, and queer theory, but there are also localized theories such as program theories, theories of change, and theories of action. Program theory is defined by Leonard Bickman as, "a plausible and sensible model of how a program is supposed to work" (1987, p. 5). Program evaluation scholars have argued that program evaluation research could be used to advance the field of knowledge when there is an explicit program theory that is confirmed or challenged with program evaluation studies. Bickman explains program theory is often classified as microtheory and macrotheory, where microtheory "provides a description of the program being evaluated" (1987, p. 6). Again, you may be saying, *What does this have to do with improvement science?* A program or intervention is usually designed to address some problem of practice; the theory behind it tells you how it is supposed to do address it. Sometimes, external program evaluators have the task of trying to make a theory explicit after a program has already been implemented. Improvement science endeavors to make the theory explicit before any change or intervention is implemented. Improvement science begins with theory.

Program theory is similar to the localized theory used within improvement science. Embedded in program theory there is often a theory of change and a theory of action. Elsewhere, with Dean Spaulding, I explained:

> You maybe be wondering how a theory of improvement is different from a theory of change or a theory of action, both common terms used in the educational lexicon. A theory of change explains the rationale behind a change in particular context, and a theory of action is the operationalization of the theory of change. (Spaulding & Hinnant-Crawford, 2019, p. 31)

A *theory of change* is essentially the "why" of a change, whereas the *theory of action* is the "how." Sullivan and Steward explain that a theory of change seeks to articulate and make explicit "the implicit theory of action inherent in a proposed intervention to delineate what *should* happen if the theory is correct and to identify short-, medium-, and long-term indicators of changes to provide the evidence base for evaluative judgments" (2006, p. 180). Measurement is a critically important piece of assessing whether a theory's tenets hold true.

A *theory of improvement* is a localized theory that explains the why and how of a particular intervention considering the system that is producing the problem, the knowledge of those who will implement the intervention, and general theories and empirical research on the problem. Bryk et al. (2015) explain the best theories of improvement come at the intersection of "three voices," which include knowledge of the system, knowledge of theory and research in the field about the problem, and knowledge of the people on the ground who will carry out whatever intervention in proposed (p. 73). When you try to make changes in a complex organization and you do not know how the system works and what is connected to what— you end up with unintended (and often detrimental) consequences.

As stated before, your theory of improvement answers the question, *What change might I introduce and why?* Your theory of improvement will be informed by your theory of knowledge; your theory of knowledge informs the "why." Bennett and Provost (2015) define a *theory of knowledge* as "a view of what theory and ideas are empirically relevant for managing and improving the system of interest" (p. 38). This is where experts and empirical research come into the improvement science process. It is essential to capitalize on what is already known. In the *90-Day Cycle Handbook* distributed by the Carnegie Foundation for the Advancement of Teaching, improvement scientists suggest doing an extent scan of the scholarly literature. This is different from the exhaustive literature review you would conduct for a dissertation or some large-scale study. I advise you to use literature in three ways throughout this process:

a. To help define, refine, and conceptualize the problem and its contributors
b. To identify potential interventions to address the problem, and
c. To identify methodological or analytical procedures to help test the change

In developing a change, literature can be quite helpful for identifying changes that have worked in other places. When examining literature, it may be difficult to access to what you need if you are not affiliated with a university library. Google Scholar and other free databases will show you thousands of results, but you may not have access to most of what you find. Begin by looking for a recent literature review or meta-analysis on your problem of practice. A recent literature review or meta-analysis will summarize the relevant literature and bring you up to speed more quickly, especially when you have limited resources you can devote to finding literature.

Collectively, what you know about your system, your stakeholders, and your theory of knowledge will determine your degree of belief in your theory of improvement. Walter A. Shewart is credited with the development of the concept "degree of belief" (Langley et al., 2009). Your degree of belief is influenced by two key factors: whether your change has worked elsewhere and how similar your context is to where it works. In essence, your degree of belief is determined by the generalizability of the empirical research on your proposed change and its generalizability to your context. And when you think about generalizability to your context, you cannot neglect the nuances of your system.

When the primary goal is improvement of processes or outcomes, the longstanding, empirically supported theory is informative, but not necessarily instructive on what you should do. You need a local theory that captures the nuances of your context, the expertise of your stakeholders, and the empirical literature on what has worked. While distinct, it is similar to theories used in program evaluation.

Table 6.1. Definitions of Localized Theories

Type of Theory	Description
Program Theory	How a program should work
Theory of Change	Why a change is warranted
Theory of Action	How a change should be implemented
Theory of Knowledge	Knowledge necessary to determine the best intervention
Theory of Improvement	Acknowledges the system that produces a particular outcome and how a change may impact (a component of) the system to improve the outcome

A Tool for Illustrating Your Theory of Improvement

A theory of improvement is a hypothesis that you will test during your iterative research cycles, called Plan-Do-Study-Act (PDSA) cycles (there is more to come on these in the following chapter). As stated above, this theory illustrates what you know about the system as well as what mechanisms you think you can change to bring about desired outcomes. A *driver diagram* is a tool that illustrates your theory of improvement. It contains your desired outcomes, key parts of the system that influence your desired outcome, and possible changes that will yield desirable results. A driver diagram looks like an organizational chart turned on its side. It has four or five major levels: the aim, the primary drivers, the secondary drivers, the change ideas, and sometimes people have a fifth level that notates change concepts.

Figure 6.1. Components of a Driver Diagram

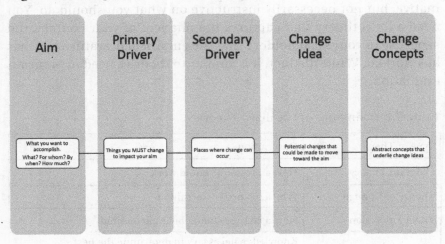

The *aim statement* is a succinct but detailed description of the desired outcome. It is the head of the driver diagrams. Aim statements are similar to SMART goals, which are specific, measurable, achievable, relevant, and timebound. An aim statement typically answers the following four questions:

1. What?
2. For whom?
3. By when?
4. How much?

These questions align to some degree with the components of SMART goals. The *what* and *for whom* make the statement specific and relevant. *By when* makes it time bound. *How much* makes it measurable.

After you have developed a clear aim, you will use information gathered in your exploration of the system to determine which parts of the system are likely to influence your aim. These parts of the system are illustrated in the second level of the diagram as primary drivers. A "driver" is defined by the Oxford English Dictionary as "one who drives" and also as, "a part of machinery, usually a wheel, which communicates motion to other parts or to which the power is directly communicated." ("driver," 2019). In each definition, you see the driver as something that steers and impacts direction. The *drivers (primary and secondary)* in a driver diagram illustrate elements of a system that influence your desired outcome: your aim. These elements are described by Bennett & Provost (2015) as "structures that comprise the system, processes that represent the work of the system and operating norms that demonstrate the explicit and tacit culture of the system" (p. 39). They go on to say that primary drivers are "high-level elements in the system that must change to accomplish the outcome of interest" and secondary drivers are "places or opportunities within the system where a change can occur" (Bennett & Provost, 2015, p. 40).

After you identify your primary and secondary drivers, you map onto them specific change ideas. *Change ideas* explain how a change will work is the pre-identified system—*your system*. Bennett and Provost (2015) describe them as tangible and specific. You may develop change ideas (during a brainstorming session) to impact specific primary or secondary drivers, but due to the nature of complex systems, "there may not be a one-to-one relationship between change ideas and the drivers the ideas might affect . . . a single idea may affect multiple drivers" (Bennett & Provost, 2015, p. 41). You will read more about developing changes later in this chapter.

The final piece of the driver diagram is the level entitled *change concepts*. As you develop a menu of change ideas, you may begin to notice that some of the ideas, while not exactly the same, have the same underlying concepts. In your organization, you may find in your menu of change ideas three or four are related to better communication. Bennett and Provost (2015) explain that change concepts "enhance the improvement journey by reflecting an abstract form that can manifest through a variety of specific change ideas" (p. 41). If communication was the underlying change concept of your change idea, and the specific change idea failed, you could try subsequent change ideas that also deal with communication. If all of the ideas dealing with communication fail, Bennett and Provost suggest it may be time to revise your theory.

Imagine you are the Vice President for Student Success at North-West South-East College (NWSEC). Your institution grants certificates, associates, and bachelor's degrees. Your face-to-face enrollment has declined over the past decade, and your degree offerings and certificate programs are increasingly going online. However, not unlike other institutions, you have a 20% lower retention rate in your online courses than in your face-to-face courses, and sometimes between 40 and 60% of your online students withdraw within the semester (Bawa, 2016). With online enrollment increasing and face-to-face enrollment decreasing, success in online courses will determine the success of NWSEC.

You convene a group of stakeholders that includes online students, faculty, academic support personnel (including the director of the tutoring center), your learning management system (LMS) administrator, and an institutional researcher—who can help illuminate and provide data on various things your committee has questions about. Collectively, after a root cause analysis and creating a system map, you begin to construct the following driver diagram.

A run chart has shown over the past 16 quarters (four years) your retention rate in online courses has been relatively stable around 52% percent. That means 52% of students who enroll at the beginning of the semester in online courses complete those courses. You begin by developing your aim statement. Collectively, you all agree on the following:

What?	*Improve retention*
For whom?	*Students in online courses*
By when?	*Next quarter*
How much?	*12%*

From the questions above, you all develop a fairly straightforward aims statement:

Increase retention in online courses by 12% next quarter.

Figure 6.2. Diagram of Aim Statement

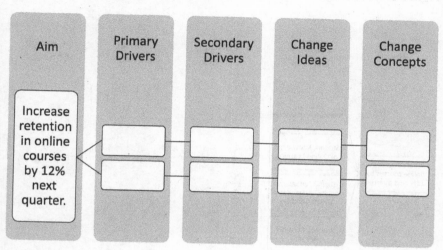

You all have also done a fair amount of reading on retention in online courses. You found a literature review of online retention entitled "Retention in Online Courses: Exploring Issues and Solutions—A Literature Review by Papia Bawa," and you shared it with your team. The review made you all aware of dominant theories related to online teaching and learning, as well as some things that may be playing into the retention problem at NWSEC.

Taking into account what you read and the expertise of the students and faculty on your team, you came up with the following as primary drivers: the learning management system (LMS), student knowledge of online learning, digital pedagogy or faculty knowledge of online teaching, and student personal factors.

Figure 6.3. Primary Drivers

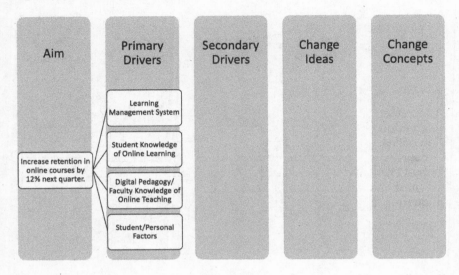

You guys thought carefully and critically about the secondary drivers because these are places or opportunities for change. When looking at the LMS, the LMS administrator said you could influence the tool available (i.e., discussion boards, journals, wikis, collaboration software, podcasts, etc.) or the layout of the virtual classroom. In terms of student knowledge and learning, the literature and the students spoke in detail about their expectations for online courses and the sense of being overwhelmed. Bawa's (2016) article explained that students often underestimate what is required in an online course because they know the face-to-face aspect is not there. Bawa (2016) also explains cognitive load may differ in the online setting "where learners are intimidated by the large amount of information that needs to be processed all at once before real learning can begin" (p. 4). In terms of digital pedagogy, it became clear that faculty were unaware how students in online courses tended to differ from students in their face to face classes. These students were more likely to be working and have families, and in some cases, be older than their face-to-face students. Faculty were also trying to essentially "put their face-to-face class online" and were unaware of best practice in creating online course content. Last but not least, they thought about the daily and extemporaneous demands on students' lives and how they may impact retention as well. Their list of secondary drivers included LMS layout and tool availability, student expectations and cognitive load, faculty knowledge of students and of content delivery, and student jobs and family obligations.

Figure 6.4. Secondary Drivers

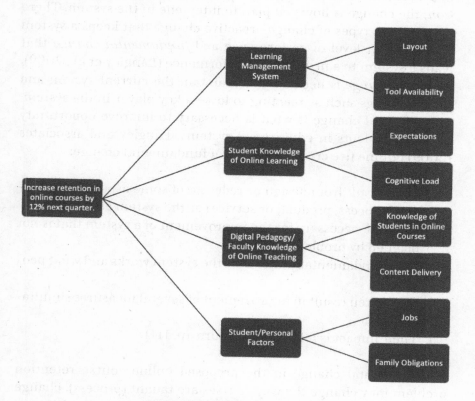

Developing Change Ideas

If an improvement scientist suffers from solutionitis, this is where the improvement process starts. Educational practitioners have no shortage of change ideas. But when your development of change ideas is scaffolded by your knowledge of the problem and the inner workings of the system, you are more likely to select a change that will actually result in an improvement.

What do improvement scientists mean when they say the word *"change?"* Langely et al. (2009) make it clear that "change is defined as the process or result of making or becoming different . . . But 'different' is not the same as 'improvement'" (p. 111). All improvement requires change, but all change does not lead to improvement. Change is often used interchangeably with *intervention;* the change is how you plan to intervene in the system. There are different types of change—reactive change that keeps a system at its present level of performance and *fundamental change* that leads a system to a new level of performance (Langley et al., 2009). *Reactive change* is necessary to maintain the current system and include things such as reacting to loss—a key player in the system. Fundamental change is what is necessary to improve opportunity gaps for students in educational systems. Langley and associates (2009) outline five critical features of fundamental change:

1. They result from design or redesign of some aspect of the system (process, product, or service) or the system as a whole.
2. They are necessary for the improvement of a system that is not plagued by problems.
3. They fundamentally alter how the system works and what people do.
4. They often result in improvement of several measures simultaneously.
5. Their impact is felt into the future. (p. 114)

A fundamental change in the proposed online course retention problem may change the way courses are taught (process), change how students interact with the LMS (what people do and how it works), and may not only increase retention, but grades within the courses. These are possible outcomes of fundamental change.

To develop fundamental changes, Langley and colleagues (2009) say you need to think logically about the current system, learn from others doing it well, think creatively, use technology, and utilize change concepts (p. 120). Langley et al. (2009) give a complete list of 72 change concepts derived from improvement methodologies like Lean and Six Sigma in *The Improvement Guide* (p. 132). This primer speaks at length about exploring the current system, so there is no need to rehash that here. The next suggestion they make is for improvement scientists to learn from others. In learning from others doing the work, Langley and associates use the term benchmarking, which they define as "merely looking around at how others are doing things and trying to learn new approaches and possibilities" (p. 123). This idea is not foreign in education; in higher education, faculty conducting peer-reviews are not only a tool for feedback for the faculty member being reviewed, but a tool for the reviewer to see new approaches to instruction. In K–12, it is also common for teachers to observe master teachers or for groups to travel to other schools to see how they are implementing some new innovation.

In this case, the team at NWSEC may visit a sister institution and view what they have implemented to increase online retention. Or they may survey sister institutions to see if they have any guidance for online teaching. In doing such, they may discover that Quality Matters and the Community of Inquiry frameworks used together lead to better online course outcomes. This may lead to one change idea.

Technology, in the sense of fundamental change, does not mean computers and tablets and wireless devices. It is a more inclusive term that can refer to "the practical application of science, including equipment, materials, information systems, and methods" (Langley et al., 2009, p. 125). If they develop an intervention to modify instructional methods or to modify the learning management system—they have moved into the realm of technology.

Thinking creatively to develop change is essential when trying not to do more of the same. Many improvement scientists embrace *design thinking* as a method to generate change ideas. Brown (2008) described design thinking "metaphorically as a system of spaces rather than a predefined series of orderly steps" (p. 4). The three spaces are inspiration—which can come from a problem of practice, ideation—the generation and testing of ideas and potential solutions, and implementation. The tools that aid in design thinking are endless. The Luma Foundation (2012) has published a great handbook to guide you through activities for collaborative design thinking, *Innovating for People: Handbook of Human-Centered Design Methods.*

Recommended Addition for the Improvement Scientist's Bookshelf

Brown says a design thinker is empathetic (can see things from the perspectives of multiple stakeholders) and uses integrative thinking. They are optimistic and are willing to go in totally new directions; they value collaboration. Integrative thinking is what Langley and associates call logical positive and logical negative/critical thinking. *Logical positive thinking* focuses on how to get a new idea to work; whereas the *logical negative thinking* focuses on finding problems and setbacks that may come with the new idea. You need to be able to think through both.

One key to generating change ideas is that nothing is off the table during the creative process of generating ideas. Later on, you will select what you will implement to try to bring about fundamental (or reactive) change, but in the initial stages, every idea counts. Ideas can come from other places, the scholarly literature, or brainstorming. But the ideas you generate need to make sense in your system. In the case of NWSEC, the team generated the ideas below to increase retention in online courses.

Figure 6.5. Change Ideas

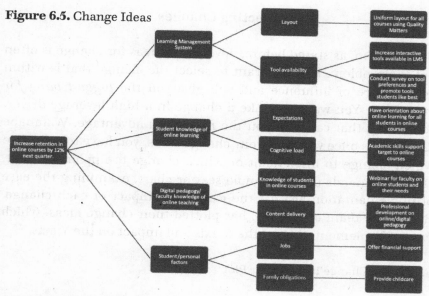

They have ideas to change the LMS, ideas to impact student knowledge, ideas to impact digital pedagogy, and ideas to change personal factors. If you examine their ideas closely, you will find three are around a particular change concept: education or capacity building.

Figure 6.6. Change Concepts

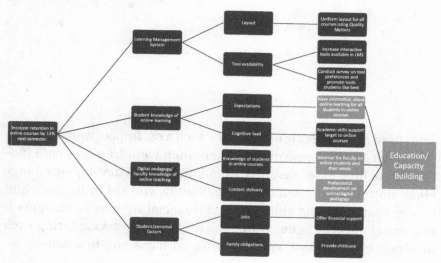

Selecting Changes

In education, as stated before, developing ideas for change is often not the problem. But you want to select the change that is within your sphere of influence and will give you the *biggest bang for your buck*. You want to make a change in a high leverage driver, something that can give you the maximum advantage. Watanabe (2009) says once you have your change ideas, you have to prioritize which change to implement or which change to implement first. He recommends using a simple scatter chart, examining the ease of implementation against the estimated impact of each change. Below, the team of NWSEC has plotted their change ideas, which ease of implementation on the X axis and impact on the Y axis.

Figure 6.7. Change Idea Scatter Plot

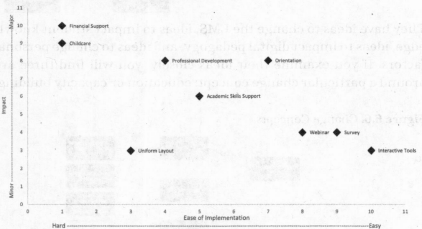

They used a simple scale of 1 to 10 for each axis. Impact went from low (1) to high (10) and ease of implementation went from low ease (difficult-1) to high ease (easy-10). Remember, when developing change ideas, nothing is thrown out. Immediately, you see in the top right corner that providing childcare and financial support to students is extremely difficult to do. Watanabe (2009) suggests exploring each quadrant of your chart, and beginning with changes in quadrant A.

Figure 6.8. Change Idea Scatter with Quadrants

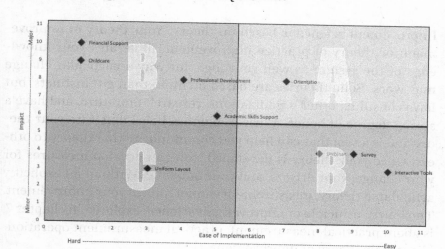

In quadrant A, you find things that are the easiest to implement but also have the greatest impact. In this case, you find Orientation. Creating an orientation for online students may help them have more realistic expectations about what successful online learning requires. The quadrants marked as B would be the next to implement. In the lower B quadrant, you find things that are easy to implement but do not have the greatest impact. However, in such a case, it is possible you could do more than one, and their combined impact may be substantial. In the case of a webinar for faculty, it would be easy to host, but the impact may be minimal because you cannot require faculty (especially tenured faculty) to attend. In the upper B quadrant, you have items that would have great impact but are more difficult to implement. The tutoring center already offers academic skills support, things such as time management, note taking, etc. However, most online tutoring has focused only on content. It would take a team in the tutoring center to do some research and train tutors to be academic skills coaches. Also, the impact is not as great as an orientation, because unlike orientation, academic skills coaching would be something students had to opt into. This chart is not magic, but it can help scaffold your thinking about how to prioritize the many solutions your team generates.

Summary

Improvement science is based on theory. Your theory of improvement, or theory of practice improvement, illustrates your knowledge of the system as well your logic for why a particular change may work. Solid theories are based on more than gut instincts, but have consulted other organizations, research literature, and have a strong degree of belief. A driver diagram helps illustrate your theory and is a tool that can help you communicate that theory to others. Once your theory is developed, you can develop measures for your change, your drivers, and your outcome. Without an explicitly articulated theory, measurement cannot inform your improvement. The fourth principle of improvement science, explored in chapter 7, is about practical measurement; practical measurement operationalizes your theory of improvement.

Key Terms

- **Aim**—An aim statement is a succinct description of the desired outcomes that answers the questions: What? For whom? By when? By how much?
- **Change**—Change is the act of making or becoming different. All improvement requires change; all change is not an improvement.
- **Change concept**—Change concepts are categories that capture multiple change ideas and show underlying approaches to systematic change.
- **Change Idea**—A change idea is an idea about how to generate change in your current system.
- **Design thinking**—Design thinking is one of many methods used to generate ideas for change and improvement. It can be viewed as three distinct phases: inspiration, ideation, and implementation.
- **Driver diagram**—A driver diagram is a tool that illustrates the theory of improvement (also known as a theory of practice improvement) that contains the desired outcomes, key parts of

the system that influence the outcome, and possible changes that will yield desirable results.

- **Drivers**—Drivers are elements within a system that influence the desired outcome, or aim.
- **Fundamental change**—Fundamental change is change that leads the system to a new (hopefully more desirable) level of performance.
- **Intervention**—Intervention is often synonymous with change; it is how you plan to intercede in the system to create improvement.
- **Logical negative thinking**—Logical negative thinking is critical in nature; it focuses on potential barriers and setbacks to implementing a new change.
- **Logical positive thinking**—Logical positive thinking is optimistic in nature; it focuses on how to get new ideas to work.
- **Reactive change**—Reactive change is change that is necessary to maintain the system's current level of performance.
- **Theory of action**—A theory of action is a localized theory that explains how a change should happen in a particular context.
- **Theory of change**—A theory of change is a localized theory that explains why a change should happen in a particular context.
- **Theory of improvement**—A theory of improvement is a localized theory that explains the why and how of a particular intervention, considering the system that is producing the problem, the knowledge of those who will implement the intervention, and dominant theories and empirical research on the problem.
- **Theory of knowledge**—A theory of knowledge outlines the theories and subject matter knowledge necessary to improve in a particular context.

Questions for Improving with Equity in Mind: Who Is Involved? Who Is Impacted?

- Will addressing our aim lead to more equitable outcomes?
- Who benefits (and who benefits *most*) from achieving this aim?
- Whose knowledge is reflected in our theory of improvement?
  - Are some stakeholders' knowledge privileged above others'?
  - Whose knowledge is absent?

- Will our change ideas lead to fundamental change?
- Is our theory of improvement based in deficit understandings of those we serve?
  - Are our change ideas focused on changing students/communities instead of changing our organization (policy, practice, processes, procedures, etc.)?

References

Bawa, P. (2016). Retention in online courses: Exploring issues and solutions—A literature review. *Sage Open, 6*(1), 2158244015621777.

Bennett, B., & Provost, L. (2015). What's Your Theory? *Quality Progress, 48*(7), 36.

Bickman, L. (1987). The functions of program theory. *New Directions for Program Evaluation, 1987*(33), 5–18.

Brown, T. (2008). Design thinking. *Harvard Business Review, 86*(6), 84.

Bryk, A. S., Gomez, L. M., Grunow, A., & LeMahieu, P. G. (2015). *Learning to improve: How America's schools can get better at getting better.* Cambridge, MA: Harvard Education Press.

Langley, G. J., Moen, R. D., Nolan, K. M., Nolan, T. W., Norman, C. L., & Provost, L. P. (2009). *The improvement guide: A practical approach to enhancing organizational performance.* Hoboken, NJ: John Wiley & Sons.

Spaulding, D. & Hinnant-Crawford, B. (2019) Tools for today's educational leaders: The basic toolbox. In R. Crow, B. Hinnant-Crawford, B., & D. Spaulding (Eds.), *The educational leader's guide to improvement science: Data, designs, and cases for reflection* (pp. 13–42). Gorham, Maine: Myers Education Press.

Sullivan, H., & Stewart, M. (2006). Who owns the theory of change? *Evaluation, 12*(2), 179–199.

Watanabe, K. (2009). *Problem solving 101: A simple book for smart people.* New York, NY: Penguin.

CHAPTER SEVEN

Operationalizing Your Theory with Practical Measurement

In chapter 2, you learned that one of the propositions of improvement science is that improvement science requires operational definitions. You may also remember that Deming defined an operational definition as "a procedure agreed upon for translation of a concept into measurement of some kind" (Deming, 1994, p. 105). This chapter is about operationalizing our definitions of improvement. Practical measurement operationalizes your theory of improvement. As a scholar-practitioner and improvement champion, you have to ask yourself: What does improvement mean in the context of this problem of practice? What does "better" look like? *How will I know my change is an improvement?* Carefully constructed measures, employed, collected, and analyzed (through the PDSA cycle) will answer that essential improvement science question.

Bryk and associates (2015) state the fourth principle for improvement science as "we cannot improve at scale what we cannot measure" (p. 14). Measurement alone does not lead to improvement, but it informs your action along the way. Because improvement science addresses problems of practice from a systems perspective, to really understand the impact of improvement, you have to measure various

135

parts of the system. Langley and associates (2009) explain in *The Improvement Guide* that "in complex projects, multiple measures are almost always needed to understand the impact of changes on components of the system and on the system as a whole" (p. 77). While decision-making in improvement science is data driven, improvement science is explicit about the kinds and types of data you need in order to improve. The authors of *Learning to Improve* state quite succinctly, "Improvement research requires gathering data about the specific processes targeted for change, intermediate outcomes directly linked to these processes, and other key markers on the pathway toward achieving the network's ultimate aims" (2015, p. 15).

Educators in general know a great deal about assessment and data. However, we are often considered DRIP: Data Rich and Information Poor. The type of data you collect and have access to plays a role in the degree to which you can make substantial improvement, Hess and Fullerton write in *Phi Delta Kappan*, an article entitled "The Numbers We Need." While primarily speaking about K-12 school districts, they argue in order to have data that informs management (i.e., decisions and improvement), there are six necessities:

1. The accurate collection of basic data [This data includes enrollment, attendance, spending, and payroll information.]
2. Data linked across time [Student identifiers often change over time.]
3. Customer service and satisfaction data
4. Data with sufficient granularity to illuminate units and activities within departments
5. Data connected across content areas
6. Providing data in real time (pp. 666–667)

Hess and Fullerton go on to say that data are necessary in six domains: student outcomes, people and things (staff positions, organizational assets), finance (how dollars are actually spent), instruction and curricular operations (who gets professional development and is it effective), human capital operations (quality of the applicant pool, how quickly are they screened), and business operations

(2009, pp. 667–668). Full disclosure: as a former data fellow for Harvard's Center for Education Policy Research Strategic Data Project, I subscribe to their triangular framework, which asserts that the right data, with the right people, can lead to the right decisions. Included in that is the idea that the people are amenable and will be informed and swayed by the data they collect. It is hard to review data that says your organization is not serving a group of students well, but instead of being resistant to that finding, you must see it as an opportunity to improve and do better.

To get the right data, you need the right measurement. In education, we encounter three types of measurement: measurement for accountability, measurement for research, and measurement for improvement (Bryk et al., 2015; Yeager, Bryk, Muhich, Hausman & Morales, 2013). *Measurement for accountability* comes with rewards and sanctions as a result of what is measured. Accountability can often be a detriment to improvement, despite its intention. Accountability measures are usually collected at the end of some cycle where it is too late to improve. Those being measured often see the measurement as primarily for judgment and not as a tool for constructive feedback. Because of the proliferation of accountability measures, many educational stakeholders are suspicious of the intention of all data collected. Deming explained, "No one, child or grown-up, can enjoy learning if he must constantly be concerned about grading and gold stars for his performance. Our educational system would be improved immeasurably by abolishment of grading. No one can enjoy his work if he will be ranked with others" (Deming, 1994, p. 110). No one is willing to learn from failure when they are fearful of failure's consequences.

Hess and Fullerton (2009) explain that in our current system, the data we rely on will not aid us in our ability to improve:

> Student achievement data alone will not allow organizations to diagnose problem and manage improvement. If math scores are disappointing, why is that? Is professional development the problem? Is hiring? It's as if a CEO's management dashboard consisted of one item—the stock price. In fact, given the state of most student achievement data systems, the better analogy is to last year's stock price. (p. 666)

While we have mastered collecting accountability data, it is divorced from learning—informing student learning and organizational learning. This data alone will help you improve—even though it can indicate a need for improvement. *Measurement for research* collects data on observable or latent variables for the purpose of modeling cause an effect for prediction or explanation. Measures for research include long batteries designed to measure a single construct, and are not designed for practical embedded usage on a regular basis. This type of measurement is used to help researchers develop and test theories.

Practical Measurement

Measurement for improvement is also often referred to as *practical measurement*. Practical measurement is practical in many ways; not only does it inform improvement, but the collection of the data is embedded in day-to-day work tasks and should not be an added burden to what people already have to do. Practical measurement is also written in the language of the context; it is designed with the user in mind. Practical measurement operationalizes the various components in the theory of improvement. By creating driver measures, your team comes to an understanding of what it means to have growth in a particular driver. You cannot develop practical measures without a theory of improvement. Without a theory about what may change before you see change in your outcomes, it is impossible to develop intermediary measures. Practical measures are collected frequently, and analyzed soon after collection, so the data yielded can inform next steps. Practical measures are pragmatic, and they break down the question of what works into four additional questions:

1. Did it work?
2. Is it working?
3. How is it working?
4. Is it working as intended? (Hinnant-Crawford, 2019)

Did it work? is answered by a lagging indicator known as an outcome measure. *Is it working?* is answered by a leading indicator known as a driver measure—which measures the intermediary goals of an improvement initiative. *How is it working?* is answered by process measures or measures of fidelity. Last but not least, *is it working as intended?* is answered by balancing measures, which makes sure there are no unintended consequences as the result of some change.

Economists and businesspersons use the language of leading and lagging indicators. They can also be used to describe measures of improvement. If you are trying to lose weight, the number on the scale is a lagging indicator. It only lets you know if you have lost weight, gained weight, or maintained your current weight. On the other hand, if you use MyFitnessPal and track your calories and use MapMyFitness to track your exercise (walking/running/biking), the data provided by those apps are leading measures. *Leading measures* help you track progress and predict lagging measures. *Lagging measures* tell you if you have been successful or not. Most of the time, accountability data consists of lagging measures.

Outcome Measures—Did it Work?

Outcome measures are the measures we are all familiar with. Notice it is the only practical measurement question, and it takes a past tense of the auxiliary verb: did. Outcomes come after the fact. Common education indicators such as summative test scores, graduation rates and retention rates would all be considered outcome measures. Outcome measures are measured infrequently, and often measured once there is nothing that can be done to change them. Outcome measures are important for indicating the success of an organization or a system; however, they do not help much in improvement except for signifying where one needs to improve. Your outcome measure is probably readily available and something your institution already tracks.

Driver Measures—Is it Working?

Driver measures let you know if you are moving in the right direction before you have the data from the outcome measure. They are leading indicators, as opposed to lagging indicators, and should have predictive validity and be able to predict the outcome measure. If asking the age-old question: what comes first, the chicken or the egg, your theory of improvement should illustrate your belief about what comes first. And whatever comes first, you have to measure the degree to which you are making progress in that area.

Driver measures are collected more frequently than outcomes measures, but not as frequently as process measures. As such, you may be able to use a longer instrument to assess progress on a driver than you could use to assess progress in a particular process. That being the case, you may want to select a previously established (psychometrically validated) instrument to measure your driver. You can use the instrument in its entirety or a subscale of the instrument that really measures the construct of interest. You can use databases like ERIC or PsychTESTS to find instruments created by scholars on a variety of latent constructs—such as motivation, efficacy, and stress. You can search the outcome of interest in a database in conjunction with keywords such as instrument, questionnaire, scale, test, survey, and measure to find out what may already exist that measures your driver.

Suppose you were the Vice President for Student Affairs at Absolute Best College (ABC) and you were concerned about the turnover rate of student affairs professionals on your campus. You know on average 50 to 60% of student affairs professionals leave the profession in the first five years (Marshall, Gardner, Hughes & Lowery, 2016), and you understand why, but you need to decrease your annual turnover rate of 30% because recruitment, hiring, and training costs are really straining your budget. You have implemented several interventions to mitigate the turnover, and one of your primary drivers is feelings of burnout. To assess this driver, you use the Maslach Burnout Inventory (MBI), which has been used with your population before (Howard-Hamilton, Palmer, Johnson

& Kicklighter, 1998). While the scale has 22 items, you only administer the nine-item subscale on Emotional Exhaustion, because that is what your intervention targeted, and you want to see the degree to which you are making progress. Your theory suggests if you decrease emotional exhaustion (a measure for burnout), you will decrease turnover. Feelings of burnout is your driver measure; turnover is your outcome.

Process Measures—How Is it Working?

Process measures are often the most difficult for educators to identify and create. For so long, educators have focused primarily on measuring outcomes, and measurement for accountability, that this seemingly new and critical piece of measurement is difficult to wrap our heads around. When a new change has been implemented, you have to identify the degree to which it was implemented as intended. Process measures are measures of fidelity.

Measures of processes can include surveys, checklists, rubrics, and/or observation protocols. You can examine a process map and determine if there are certain points in the process where you need to inspect or measure the flow. Process measures are collected frequently, so you can detect variation and deviation in the process from what is desired. Because they are collected frequently (daily, bi-weekly, etc.), they cannot be time-consuming and difficult to complete. They should be able to fit into people's everyday routines without disruption. When developing process measures, think about who is in the best position to collect the data. If you are seeking to understand pedagogy, you may ask teachers to identify their methods *or* ask students to recall what they remember happening. In general, the best way to collect data on what happens in the classroom is through observations, though that can be time-consuming and laborious. If you have administrators already conducting walk-throughs or a peer-review process already in place, and you are looking for specific pedagogical techniques, it is best to attach observational data collection to observations already taking place.

Implementation scientists provide guidance on how to think about measuring processes and fidelity to intervention design. Implementation science suggests the necessity of a measure of adherence. Carroll and associates (2007) explain adherence as:

> "An evaluation to gauge how much of the intervention's prescribed content has been delivered, how frequently, and for how long. However, adherence may not require every single component of an intervention to be implemented. An intervention may also be implemented successfully, and meaningfully, if only the "essential" components of the model are implemented" (p. 5).

You have to determine which components of a process are essential and how best to measure them.

In her well-known 1995 article "But That's Just Good Teaching: The Case for Culturally Relevant Pedagogy," Gloria Ladson-Billings defines culturally relevant pedagogy as pedagogy that allows students to do three things: "(a) Students must experience academic success; (b) students must develop and/or maintain cultural competence; and (c) students must develop critical consciousness through which they challenge the status quo of the current social order" (p. 160). If culturally relevant pedagogy was an intervention, all three of the above must be present in order for it to be implemented with fidelity. Nineteen years later, in 2014, Ladson-Billings wrote *Culturally Relevant Pedagogy 2.0 a.k.a. the Remix*, where she embraces the evolution of culturally sustaining pedagogy (Paris, 2012), and explains while she appreciates how people have latched on to cultural relevant pedagogy, time and time again, they leave out one of the essential three. Ladson-Billings elucidates:

> Despite the apparent popularity of culturally relevant pedagogy, I have grown increasingly dissatisfied with what seems to be a static conception of what it means to be culturally relevant . . . few have taken up the sociopolitical dimensions of the work, instead dulling its critical edge or omitting it altogether . . . I could see teachers who had good intentions . . . However, they rarely pushed students to consider critical perspectives on policies and practices that may have direct impact on their lives and communities. There was no discussion of issues such as school choice, school closings, rising incarceration rates, gun laws, or

even everyday school climate questions like whether students should
wear uniforms (which typically sparks spirited debate). (pp. 77_78)

In determining the fidelity to the design, teachers who omit one of the
essential three are not adhering to the tenants of culturally relevant pedagogy. So, if one was designing a process measure for culturally relevant
pedagogy, at a minimum one would ask if students had an opportunity
for all three aspects in a particular lesson (this example is for illustrative
purposes; this is not to essentialize culturally relevant pedagogy).

In addition to asking if all three essential outcomes were achieved,
you might also design your process measure to collect an error count.
Using survey logic, if a respondent says one of the three was absent, a
follow-up question about the reason would appear. The follow-up question could be multiple choice or open-ended. A multiple-choice item
would allow for the creation of a Pareto chart, where you could determine if there are commonalities across classrooms for failing to achieve
one aspect. Figure 7.1 is an illustration of how the display logic appears
on the design side and the viewers side in the Qualtrics survey interface.

Figure 7.1. Display Logic in Qualtrics Survey Design

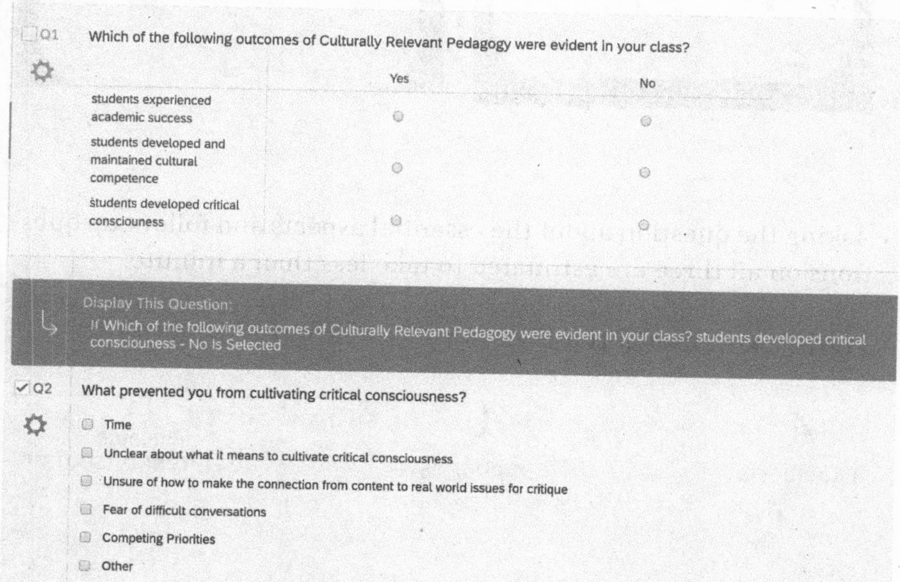

Figure 7.2. Initial Item   **Figure 7.3.** Logic Generated Item

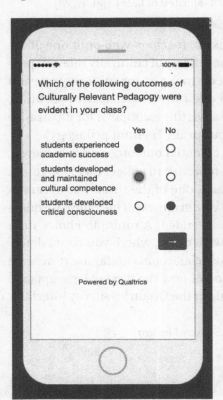
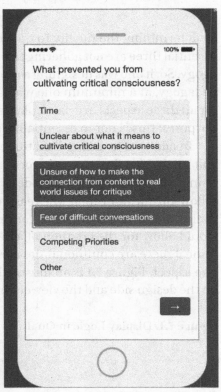

Asking the question about the essential aspects and follow-up questions on all three are estimated to take less than a minute.

Figure 7.4. Estimated Time

4	**1**	**1** minute
Questions	Languages	Est. response time

Self-report has its drawbacks. But if this was done with anonymity, respondents might be honest. If over two weeks you determine the primary reasons teachers do not attempt to cultivate cultivating critical consciousness while trying to employ culturally relevant pedagogy is because they are unclear of what it means, they are unsure of how to make connections, and they are fearful of difficult conversations in the classroom—then you can intervene to build their capacity in those areas. Process measures are essential in showing you what to do next. They let you know whether or not the change idea is ineffective or if the implementation is the problem. When we abandon interventions prematurely, and have not accessed the degree to which they were implemented we may be abandoning strategies that could improve our systems and our student's opportunities to learn.

Balancing Measures—Did it work as intended?

Balancing measures are like vital signs. They measure the overall health of the system. Your blood pressure, temperature, oxygen level, and heart rate are key signals if somebody function has gone awry or if an illness is present. However, they also serve as indicators of a reaction to a drug that may be administered to treat some problem, but has a side effect that causes another. They ensure that introducing a change in one part of the system does not disrupt or have unintended consequences on other parts of the system.

Ebony Legacy University (ELU) is a historically Black university in the southern part of the United States. Historically, ELU has focused on building its endowment through the philanthropic donations from foundations and corporations that align with the academic priorities of the institution. Like many Historically Black Colleges and Universities (HBCUs), they rely more heavily on philanthropic donations than alumni support for their endowment (Cohen, 2006). This is not because the alumni do not love and support institution. But generally, they make less money and there are fewer of them (numbers wise) than alumni from predominantly White institutions. Because the endowment is one of the indicators of fiscal health of the institution, ELU has launched a new campaign to seek alumni support as a part of their fundraising initiatives. The staff in the Office of Advancement has been tracking a number of indicators to assess the effectiveness of this initiative. They have tracked the number of alumni donors, the amounts of the donations they have received, and the number of confirmed contacts they have made with alumni. The total amount received from alumni is an outcome measure. The number of alumni donating is a driver measure, as well as the average amount per donation. The number of confirmed contacts is a process measure, assessing the actual reach of the campaign (The campaign is not working as intended if alumni do not actually know about it). While ELU's advancement office focuses on increasing the money coming in for the endowment from alumni, a balancing measure would be to ensure that their philanthropic donations have not decreased. In other words, during the course of this campaign to raise money from alumni, they would like to see their income from other philanthropic sources (corporations, foundations, and generous community donors), remain stable. Tracking their philanthropic income throughout their alumni campaign is a balancing measure.

Measurement Matters

Practical measurement is not about conducting the most sophisticated statistical analysis. It is about collecting data in a timely manner that can inform what you do next to keep you moving toward your aim. Practical measures allow you to measure different parts of complex systems and they operationalize your theory of improvement. They illuminate the pragmatic questions of what works, for whom and under what circumstances, and delineate the what works question even more by answering:

- Did it work?
- Is it working?
- How is it working?
- Is it working as intended?

We need measures that do all of the above to make informed decisions about how to improve. Measurement is critical in testing the efficacy of changes; without measurement in place, you are unable to determine the impact of change ideas. Chapter 8 deals with the penultimate improvement science principle, using disciplined inquiry to drive improvement. The next chapter will also show measurement is necessary to test change and to inform next steps.

Key Terms

- **Balancing measures**—Balancing measures are system vital signs. They are measures that ensure a change in one part of the system does not upset other parts of the system. Balancing measures answer the question: is it working as intended?
- **Driver measures**—A driver measure is an intermediary measure that can be assessed prior to the outcome. Driver measures have predictive validity for outcome measures, and measure movement in a primary or secondary driver. They answer the question: is it working?
- **Measurement for accountability**—Measurement for accountability is usually a lagging indicator, collected at the end of some cycle (academic year, term, semester). Measurement for accountability is tied to rewards and sanctions.
- **Measurement for improvement**—Measurement for improvement or practical measurement is data collected to inform improvement efforts. They operationalize the theory of improvement. Practical measures are collected frequently, embedded in day-to-day tasks, and are written in a language for various stakeholders to understand. Four practical measures are used in improvement science: outcome measures, driver measures, balancing measures, and process measures.
- **Measurement for research**—Measurement for research consists of instruments created to measure latent constructs to be used in the testing and modeling of theory. Research instruments are often characterized as being long batteries of items, with multiple items trying to assess the same latent underlying trait.

- **Outcome measures**—Outcome measures measure outcomes. They are lagging measures that answer the question: did it work?
- **Process measures**—Process measures are often measures of fidelity, ensuring process variation is under control. They answer the question: how is it working?

Questions for Improving with Equity in Mind: Who Is Involved? Who Is Impacted?

- What burden will data collection put on already taxed stakeholders?
- Are our measures assessing system processes or people?
- How have we communicated the goals of measurement for improvement?
- How will we ensure stakeholders this data is not punitive or for accountability?

References

Bryk, A. S., Gomez, L. M., Grunow, A., & LeMahieu, P. G. (2015). *Learning to improve: How America's schools can get better at getting better.* Cambridge, MA: Harvard Education Press.

Carroll, C., Patterson, M., Wood, S., Booth, A., Rick, J., & Balain, S. (2007). A conceptual framework for implementation fidelity. *Implementation Science, 2*(1), 40.

Cohen, R. T. (2006). Black college alumni giving: A study of the perceptions, attitudes, and giving behaviors of alumni donors at selected historically black colleges and universities. *International Journal of Educational Advancement, 6*(3), 200–220.

Deming, W. E. (2000/1994). *The new economics for industry, government, education.* Cambridge, MA: MIT Press.

Hess, F. M., & Fullerton, J. (2009). The numbers we need: Bringing balanced scorecards to education data. *Phi Delta Kappan, 90*(9), 665–669.

Hinnant-Crawford, B. (2019) Practical measurement. In Crow, R., Hinnant-Crawford, B., & Spaulding, D. (Eds.). *The Educational Leader's Guide* to *Improvement Science: Data, Designs, and Cases for Reflection* (pp. 43–70). Gorham, Maine: Myers Education Press.

Howard-Hamilton, M. F., Palmer, C., Johnson, S., & Kicklighter, M. (1998). Burnout and related factors: Differences between women and men in student affairs. *College Student Affairs Journal, 17*(2), 80.

Ladson-Billings, G. (1995). But that's just good teaching! The case for culturally relevant pedagogy. *Theory Into Practice, 34*(3), 159–165.

Ladson-Billings, G. (2014). Culturally relevant pedagogy 2.0: aka the remix. *Harvard Educational Review, 84*(1), 74–84.

Langley, G. J., Moen, R. D., Nolan, K. M., Nolan, T. W., Norman, C. L., & Provost, L. P. (2009). *The improvement guide: a practical approach to enhancing organizational performance.* John Wiley & Sons.

Marshall, S. M., Gardner, M. M., Hughes, C., & Lowery, U. (2016). Attrition from student affairs: Perspectives from those who exited the profession. *Journal of Student Affairs Research and Practice, 53*(2), 146–159.

Paris, D. (2012). Culturally sustaining pedagogy: A needed change in stance, terminology, and practice. *Educational Researcher, 41*(3), 93–97.

Yeager, D., Bryk, A., Muhich, J., Hausman, H., & Morales, L. (2013). Practical measurement. *Palo Alto, CA: Carnegie Foundation for the Advancement of Teaching, 78712.*

CHAPTER EIGHT

Planning, Doing, Studying, and Acting

Improvement Methodology

In the introduction of this text, I describe improvement science as a methodological framework undergirded by principles. This chapter describes the methodological aspects of the improvement science framework. Building on the previous four principles, this chapter examines principle five, which states scholar-practitioners must use disciplined inquiry to drive improvement. In a text such as this, it is tempting to jump to this chapter and begin, but as I have stated throughout the book—the principles are not steps, and you need to employ all of them to achieve improvement at scale.

This chapter is the longest chapter in the primer. Within it, I will introduce you to Langley and associates' (2009) Model for Improvement and the PDSA cycle. We will begin by tracing the origin of the PDSA inquiry model; we will juxtapose the PDSA cycle to the scientific method; we will discuss logistics for employing the method (building improvement teams, writing guiding documents), and we will explore research designs employed in the PDSA cycle. Finally, I acknowledge that this approach to improvement research is not the only approach. The latter part of the chapter introduces you to other methodological frameworks that can be used to drive improvement in education.

In chapter 6, I explained your theory of improvement begins to answer the question: *What change might I introduce and why?* Improvement methodology—which relies on practical measurement (chapter 7), aids you in determining the final essential question: *Is the change actually an improvement?*

The Model for Improvement

In *The Improvement Guide*, Langley and associates (2009) advance a Model for Improvement. They articulate, "Combined, the three questions and the PDSA cycle are the framework." The three essential questions they use to guide the process are:

1. What are we trying to accomplish? [What is our aim?]
2. How will we know that a change is an improvement? [What are our mechanisms for feedback?]
3. What change can we make that will result in an improvement? [What change can be introduced in our system to move us closer to our aim?] (p. 24)

At this point, these questions, or a derivative of them, are familiar to you. This text is organized around these essential questions and the principles of improvement—with one caveat: I focus on defining the problem before defining the aim. It is important to note, Langley and colleagues say, "The questions can be answered in any order" (p. 24). However, the questions alone are not the *Model for Improvement*; the questions in conjunction with the PDSA cycle are the Model for Improvement (see figure 8.1).

Figure 8.1. Model for Improvement

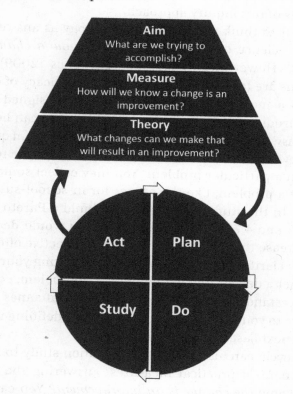

This chapter focuses on the PDSA cycle. What is a PDSA cycle, you may ask?

The PDSA Cycle

The *Plan-Do-Study-Act cycle* is described as an "efficient tri-al-and-learning methodology" (Langley et al., 2009, pp. 24–25). The foundation of the continuous improvement process is developing theory, testing that theory, and then revising that theory based on the results of those tests. But unlike traditional forms of research, this is localized theory, unique to a specific system, and narrowly focused on how to improve that system's outcomes. The iterative tests and revisions of theory are the basis for the epistemological underpinnings of this inquiry approach.

It is easiest to think about this methodology as answering the improvement science question: *How will I know a change is an improvement?* However, Langley and colleagues (2009) explain its applications are far greater than testing the efficacy of changes. Because it is a methodological process that is designed to build knowledge through iterative cycles, the PDSA cycle can be used in developing answers to each of the Model for Improvement questions.

A PDSA cycle can be used to determine your aim, or to narrow your focus on a particular problem. You may collect some data on the source of a problem, like the causes for in-school-suspensions in chapter 4. In the study phase, you may build a Pareto chart, as in figures 4.6 and 4.7. As you study them, you would decide your aim is to decrease the number of ISS due to subjective offenses like disrespect. In clarifying the problem and articulating your aim, you can plan to get a deeper understanding of the problem, collect (do) data to understand the problem, study those outcomes and how they compare to your predictions, and then act—defining the aim of what you do next based on that study.

A PDSA cycle can also serve as a validation study to help with the development of practical measures, answering the question: *How will I know the change is an improvement?* You can pilot or field-test survey items to see stakeholders' perceptions of relevance, or clarity of the items on a particular instrument. You may also want to test the reliability of a particular measure over time to see if raters begin to drift in their scoring. These types of inquiries could be undertaken under a PDSA cycle as well.

For the purpose of this primer, we will primarily look at the use of the PDSA for assessing the impact of a change, and determining whether or not a change is actually an improvement. *The Improvement Guide* gives more details (a chapter on each) of the different applications of the PDSA cycle to different processes in improvement work.

The Origins of the PDSA Cycle

The PDSA cycle has roots in manufacturing and production. In his 1939 text, *Statistical Method from the Viewpoint of Quality Control,* Walter Shewhart illustrated a cyclical model for controlling quality. He explained:

> These three steps must go in a circle instead of a straight line ... It may be helpful to think of the three steps in mass production process as steps in the scientific method. In this sense, specification, production, and inspection correspond respectively to making a hypothesis, carrying out an experiment, and testing the hypothesis. The three steps constitute a dynamic scientific process of acquiring knowledge. (1939/1986, p. 45)

Figure 8.2. Shewhart Cycle

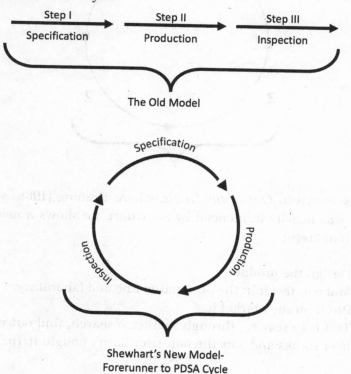

Shewhart's cycle for manufacturing was the precursor to the Plan-Do-Study-Act cycle, used widely in improvement science. W. E. Deming, a student of Shewhart, amended Shewhart's illustration to include a fourth step.

Figure 8.3. Deming Wheel

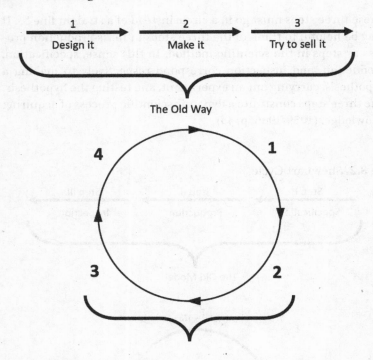

As shown in *Out of the Crisis*, where Deming (1986) says this work was heavily influenced by Shewhart, he shows a new wheel with four steps:

1. Design the product.
2. Make it; test it in the production line and laboratory.
3. Put it on the market it.
4. Test it in service; through market research, find out what the user thinks and why the non-user hasn't bought it. (p. 180)

While this is detailed in his 1986 book, Moen and Norman (2006) refer to this iteration as the Deming Wheel and date it to 1951.

In Japan, the Deming Wheel was modified after a 1950s presentation to the Union of Japanese Scientists and Engineers and the *Plan-Do-Check-Act cycle* was developed. Moen and Norman provide a crosswalk between the original wheel and the PDCA cycle:

Design	→	Plan
Production	→	Do
Sales	→	Check
Research	→	Act

Figure 8.4. Japanese PDCA

1951 Japanese PDCA Cycle
Created by Christoph Roser (2016)
AllAboutLean.com

The original PDCA has been augmented to a more robust improvement framework, referred to as *FOCUS-PDCA*. Similar to the Model for Improvement, but rather than being guided by questions, it is guided by action steps: 1. find a process to improve, 2. organize a team that knows the process, 3. clarify the current knowledge of the process, 4. understand the causes of process variation, and 5. select the process improvement. These steps lead into the PDCA cycle.

Figure 8.5. Focus PDCA

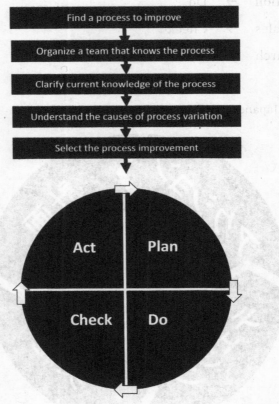

Batalden & Stoltz (1995) explain that in the medical field, FOCUS-PDCA is widely used as well as the PDCA worksheet, entitled *Building Knowledge for Improvement: A PDCA Worksheet*, which guides the process with eight precipitating questions:

1. What are we trying to accomplish?
2. How will we know that a change is an improvement?
3. What changes can we make that we predict will lead to improvement?
4. How shall we PLAN the pilot?
5. What are we learning as we DO the pilot?
6. As we CHECK and study what happened, what have we learned?
7. As we ACT to hold the gains or abandon our pilot efforts, what needs to be done?
8. Looking back over the whole pilot, what have we learned? (p. 156)

While there are similarities between the PDCA and PDSA cycles, and sometimes you find the terms used interchangeably, individuals who are knowledgeable in improvement methodologies understand there are distinctions.

In the 1980s, Deming reintroduced the Shewhart cycle with four steps and eventually began referring to it as the Plan-Do-Study-Act cycle. Deming wanted to distinguish it from the PDCA cycle, cautioning that for "Western audiences . . . the plan, do, check, act version is inaccurate because the word 'check' means 'to hold back.'" Furthermore, Taylor and colleagues (2014), explain:

> Deming was cautious over the use of the "PDCA" terminology and warned it referred to an explicitly different process, referring to a quality control circle for dealing with faults in a system, rather than the PDSA process, which was intended for iterative learning and improvement of a product or process. (p. 296)

While similarities exist, it is important to be aware of the differences, and to select the methodology that is appropriate for what you are trying to achieve.

When Deming reintroduced the Shewhart cycle in the 1980s and 1990s, he continued to refer to it as the Shewhart cycle. The 1994 version, which Deming (1994, p. 132) called the "Shewhart cycle for learning and improvement—the PDSA cycle" is the basis of the PDSA cycle in Langley et al.'s Model for Improvement (Moen & Norman, 2006).

Figure 8.6. Deming's Depiction of PDSA Cycle

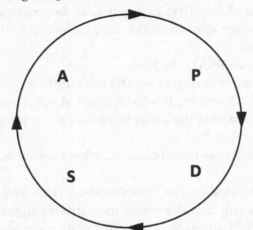

The Shewhart Cycle for Learning and Improvement
The P D S A Cycle

For a more detailed explanation of the history and evolution of the PDSA cycle, I refer the reader to the work of Moen and Norman (2006).

The Science of the PDSA Cycle

Deming called the PDSA a cycle for both learning and improvement. It is designed to build new knowledge with each additional cycle—about what works, what does not work, for whom, and under what conditions. As Shewhart suggested in 1939, his initial wheel articulated a method for developing a hypothesis and testing it; improvement science is not distinct from other science in that matter. In fact, Speroff and O'Connor (2004) argue the steps in a PDSA cycle are analogous to those in the scientific method.

Figure 8.7. PDSA and the Scientific Method

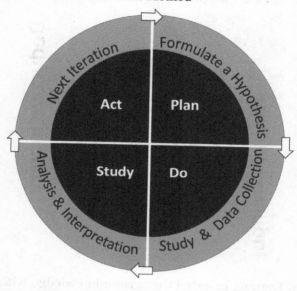

These authors explicate, as depicted in Figure 8.7, "The PDSA model advocates the formation of a hypothesis for improvement (Plan), a study protocol with collection of data (Do), analysis and interpretation of the results (Study), and the iteration for what to do next (Act)" (Speroff & O'Connor, 2004, p. 17).

Taylor, McNicholas, Nicolay, Darzi, Bell, and Reed (2014) articulate five defining features of PDSA framework: iterative cycles, prediction-based test of change, small-scale testing, use of data over time, and documentation. Unfortunately, in their literature review of the use of PDSAs in health-care, only two out of 73, or 2.7% of the studies reviewed, claimed to use all five features in outlined in the methodology.

Iterative cycles are essential to learning. Embedded in each PDSA cycle are opportunities for inductive and deductive learning. The first half of each cycle, the Plan and Do phases, illustrate a deductive approach to inquiry. A theory is developed and then tested. The latter half of the cycle is an opportunity for inductive learning. In the Study and Act portion, you move from observations or data, to clarified understandings, to revised theory.

Figure 8.8. PDSA and Inductive/Deductive Inquiry

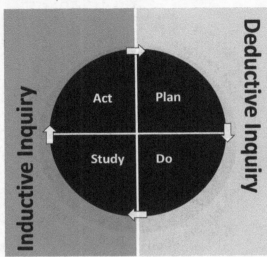

Remember, Deming asserted there is no knowledge without prediction. You begin with a theory and test it, and you end with developing or revising the theory in preparation to test it again. The process is designed to improve as well as build knowledge. Langley and associates illustrate the interplay between deductive and inductive learning below.

Figure 8.9. Inductive/Deductive Cycles

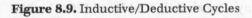

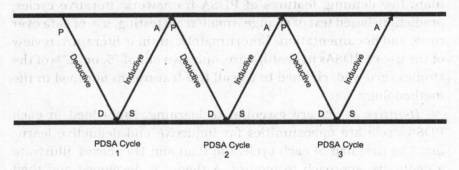

Adapted from Langley et al. (2009)

Each cycle is designed to inform the next. If only one cycle was completed, you may have used tools of improvement science, but you cannot call it improvement science. A commitment to using improvement science is a commitment to an iterative pursuit of improvement; you must acknowledge and expect that every cycle will not yield the result you want, but you will learn something. And what you learn will guide what you do next.

Small-scale tests are another critical hallmark of improvement science. You need to know if something works before you implement it on a large scale. Unfortunately, educational initiatives are usually implemented at large scale, and then wait an academic year or semester before there is any real data on how they are working. If an initiative is not working as intended, the implication is that students have been exposed to it for an extended period of time before anyone was able to act. Improvement science tries to avoid wasted time. Instead of implementing a new curriculum with all of 3rd grade, it suggests trying it in a class or two and then, when you see promise, expand further. Also, during your iterative cycles, you begin to learn how to make the intervention work. And what you learn about implementation from initial cycles informs your implementation in subsequent cycles. When thinking about where to begin small tests of change in an educational organization, think about two extremes—the naysayers and the innovators. The innovators will be assets on an improvement team during the study and act phase, thinking about what could be done differently. The naysayers will focus on everything that went wrong. Collectively, they will give you the positive logical and the negative logical thinking to inform what happens next.

If you are not examining data over time, you are probably not using improvement science. As discussed in the previous chapter, measurement is essential to improvement. It not only operationalizes what you mean by improvement, but it informs you whether your change or intervention has had some unintended consequences. If you are unaware of your system's "normal," you will have no way to illustrate improvement or detriment due to some change. Understanding variation in outcomes and processes is essential to tracking improvement. Sometimes baseline data are not available, and the necessity of a change does not allow you the luxury of building historical data. Once you have your measures in place, begin collecting immediately so you have at least some understanding of where you started. Do not let the absence of historical data deter you from taking steps to improve.

Before the PDSA

Remember, improvement science is a collaborative endeavor. As such, it is essential that a plan is laid out and key players understand the plan. The key players throughout the improvement process may change. You may have different people around the table when defining the problem than you have when you are developing a plan to implement a proposed change. If that is the case, it is your responsibility to make sure knowledge from one stage is carried over to the next. Often, improvement initiatives begin with the delineation of who is going to be on the team. In K-12 institutions, there usually is a School Improvement Team. In higher education, there are task forces and Quality Enhancement Plan (QEP) teams. Sometimes it makes sense to capitalize on the structures in place; other times, if you know the people on those teams are invested in maintaining the status quo, new teams may need to be developed.

You may choose to have a design team and an implementation team. The *design team* helps to design the intervention and will be involved through the planning stage. The implementation team carries out the work and is front and center during the do, study, and act phases. They may also be involved in subsequent planning stages because they have the knowledge of what happened in the initial phase. The degree of overlap in the teams will depend on availability and willingness to commit. It may be beneficial to have a CEO or CFO on the design team to sign off and know you have a champion who can sometimes clear the way for the work to be done. But realistically, they do not have the time nor capacity to deal with the minutia of implementing what is designed. As you determine who should be on your teams, remember to see the system, and think about whose voices should be included and whose voices are missing. As the improvement scientist, it is your responsibility to get those voices on the table. To improve for equity, you can never forget to think about who is involved and who is impacted.

Design-based implementation research considers the necessity for synergy between academics and practitioners. You will want to have subject matter experts on the design team. This can be those with success at other places and/or academics who have studied the problem at hand. They are not the most important voices, but they are critical voices in selecting good designs. If you are in a geographically isolated place and there is not a local college, university, or think tank—ask someone to join your team in a consulting fashion, remotely. Some may be willing to help because of service or commitment to the work. Others will be willing to work with you pro bono if a publication can result from the work, or if it is their passion. If you are getting expertise on your team through non-voluntary means, be sure to have a contract that is explicit about what the roles in the relationship are. And remember, while they are experts on the subject matter, all of the knowledge in the room, including those who have knowledge of the context and the problem from being closest to it, is of equal weight.

You will probably serve on both teams and function as the profound knowledge expert. You understand improvement, systems, and variation in ways others may not. You know it is essential to operationalize what we mean by making something "better" and you can lead the teams through a variety of activities with a number of tools to help them arrive at better decisions.

P-D-S-A

As stated earlier, this chapter will focus on the application of the PDSA cycle to testing the efficacy of interventions or changes that you hope lead to an improvement. The changes explored can be changes in processes, structures, or the broader systems. Langley et al. (2009) articulate three principles for testing changes: start on a small scale, collect data over time, and include a wide range of conditions in subsequent test. Using these principles leads each test to refine your theory and increase your degree of belief in the efficacy of a particular change. Thus far, we have discussed a great deal about the PDSA cycle as a whole, but what happens in each part of the cycle?

Plan

The different steps in the PDSA cycle have names that are instructive. In the planning phase—you plan. Deming described this phase as developing "a plan for a test, comparison, [or] experiment" (1994, p. 132). Langley et al. (2009) are a little more descriptive, saying the plan stage identifies objectives, articulates the questions and predictions, delineates the steps in carrying out the test (including who is responsible, the timeline, and where it will take place), and how data will be collected throughout. Most of the primer informs the planning stage or stage 0, which takes place before the planning stage. Deming explains, "Somebody has an idea for improvement of a product or process. This is the 0-th stage" (1994, pp. 131–132). Everything else in this text has led up to your being ready to develop a plan to produce improvement in your organization.

After your team has been assembled (design and/or implementation team), you want to make sure everyone is on the same page. Many of the tools discussed in the previous chapters are helpful for getting individuals on the same page and using the same language. At a minimum, if your team is full of new people, review your fishbone diagram and your driver diagram. Having the entire team understand your theory of improvement is a nonnegotiable. Langley and associates (2009) suggest developing a *charter*, a guiding document, to ensure everyone is on the same page. The charter can be delineated using the Model for Improvement—as it includes those questions as the guidance. A charter includes the following:

1. **General Description**
   The general description of the goals of the improvement effort which answers the question—*What are we trying to accomplish*? Once an aim statement has been constructed, it should

be in the charter's description. This section of the charter should also be explicit to the *what* and *why* of the improvement initiative. In your charter, you can explicitly tie your why to equitable outcomes.

2. **Predictions and Measures**
   Remember the PDSA is an exercise in testing theory, or testing your predictions. You must be explicit in what those are. List out your expected outcomes from a particular change. In this section, you must also state *how you will know the change is an improvement*. What data or indicators are you using to determine whether or not the change is an improvement. In the charter, be specific—name instruments.

3. **Procedures, Methods, Scope**
   What is the actual "do" that is going to be done? Your charter lays out a plan for the rest of the cycle. What are the activities that must be completed during and before the "Do" phase? What resources are at your disposal and what is beyond the scope of what you are doing? What is the anticipated time frame? What type of data are you collecting? How will that data be analyzed? Are your PDSAs lasting a week? Four weeks? How long into implementation does your team convene to examine how the work is going? The research design embedded to test the change is stated in this section of the charter as well.

4. **Participation**
   Who is responsible for carrying out the various activities outlined in the previous section? If something has costs or takes time, who is responsible for covering those costs or giving individuals time to complete it? Langley et al. (2009) suggest the participation section speak to members of the teams as well as sponsors of the work.

Think of the charter as a proposal or guiding protocol. It should lay out the plan and who is responsible. It should also lay out the threshold for intervening. In education, at a minimum, you must do no harm. Just as we operationalize what it means to improve, it is necessary to operationalize what would be considered a detrimental effect. If a change is a detriment, you need to indicate the level in which a change may be perceived as detrimental and your plan to intercede should that occur. The format of the charter is not critically important. It should be fairly short and accessible to anyone involved in the initiative. Do not write it for an academic audience if people involved in implementation will not be able to read it.

Do not shortchange the *P* in the PDSA cycle. There is a reason it is first; everything else rests on its foundation. Deming (1994) warns, "A hasty start may be ineffective, costly, and frustrating. People have a weakness to short-circuit this step. They cannot wait to get into motion, to be active to look busy, move into Step 2 [Do]" (p. 132). The planning is essential for a smooth cycle.

Do

Most of the work, in figuring out this phase, is done in the planning phase. Deming explains in the do phase you "carry out the test, comparison, or experiment, preferably on a small scale, according to the layout decided in step 1" (1994, p. 133). The do phase is a combination of implementation and documentation of what is happening. Langley and associates (2009) describe the do phase as consisting of three parts: executing the plan, documenting what happens, and initializing the analysis of the data collected. While to many, improvement science appears to be a heavily quantitative enterprise, to be done well, ethnographic data is also collected during the do phase. In essence, everyone involved with implementation in a participant observer. You are participating in an intervention, but simultaneously, you have to be keenly aware of what is happening. While you have measures to determine the impact on different parts of the system, you have to be prepared to document the unexpected. There has to be a mechanism for note-taking. In your measures, such as surveys or checklists, you can always add an open-ended item for additional observations. You could ask participants to journal, make notes, create voice memos, or video diaries about their experiences during implementation. Depending on the nature of the initiative and who is involved, you may also be able to leverage social media as a method of data collection. You could have a weekly Twitter chat with a unique hashtag where people report what went wrong or went right with a particular intervention (particularly if this was a part of a large network implementing a change). In ethnographic research, there is an axiom that if it is not in the field notes, then it did not happen. Documentation of the process is important for building knowledge and driving improvement.

Documentation is not confined to the do phase, but if not considered a priority, it is easy to overlook. In *The Improvement Guide*, in Appendix B, Form B.3 is a PDSA cycle form with prompts to ask yourself throughout each part of the cycle—and open-ended boxes for observations during the do phase. During the do phase, you are collecting many kinds of data. Some data will inform your process and will require being analyzed as a part of the do phase. If you have collected data daily or weekly to build a run chart, you may want to go on and build that chart and add each new bit of information as it comes in, instead of waiting to the end of the cycle to compile it.

Study

The study cycle is just that, an opportunity to reflect on what happened during the do phase. In the study phase of the cycle, you compare the predictions articulated during the planning phase to what actually happened. You may ask yourself and your team:

- Did this go as we expected? Were our predictions close?
- What happened that was unexpected?
- What conditions could have influenced our outcome?

During this phase, you analyze the data, and if necessary, compare data after implementation of the change to data prior to implementation of the change. You also question the sufficiency of your data. Did the data collected answer the questions posed? Is there another indicator you should consider during the next cycle?

The study phase is not a time for insular, individual reflection. It is a time of collaborative meaning making of the process that took place. Document the meaning-making done during the study phase with a summary of what was learned. You can review and revise your fishbones, driver diagrams, system, or process maps to reflect the new learning from the initial cycle.

Act

While every research article has implications for practice or suggestions for further research, the act portion of the PDSA cycle is really what makes it different. You begin a PDSA with the understanding that it is going to be one phase in an iterative process, and what you learn from this phase will inform what you do next. Typically, there are five actions at the end of a PDSA cycle: adopt, adapt, expand, abandon, or test again under other conditions.

The act phase bleeds into the next plan phase if done correctly. In the act phase you use what you learned from the study phase to figure out how to move forward. The documentation of the unexpected and the summary of things learned should help you to move forward in a more informed manner. If a change leads to an improvement, you may adopt it and run it again to see if it continues to work or if the initial benefits diminish. You may find it did not work as intended but believe if you tweak some aspect of the initiative (adapt), it will yield the results you want. Again, this leads to another cycle. If you believe the change was detrimental, you may decide to abandon it or modify it extensively before testing it again. If it worked well in one area, you may try to expand it to another grade-level or program. At the culmination of the act phase, you should be developing the objectives of the next cycle.

Figure 8.10. Continual PDSA Cycles

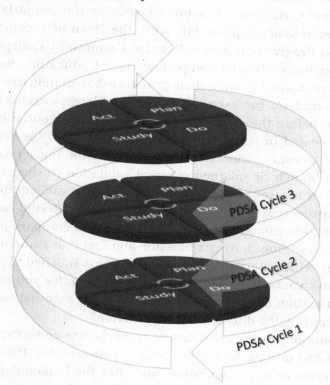

Each cycle adds knowledge as you learn while you do. The knowledge of the problem of practice and how to address it grows with each iteration.

Selecting Research Design Within the PDSA

Research design informs the PDSA cycle. Research is embedded within the PDSA cycle. In the planning phase, you have to determine the research design that will be employed because it will be carried out in the do phase. Langley et al. (2009) give four omnibus research designs to be considered when testing changes: observational, before and after, time series, and factorial designs.

The *observational design*, to some degree, is similar to a quasi-experiment, without a baseline illustrating the similarly of the groups beforehand. Suppose you were the Dean of Technical and Vocational Programs at Access Granted Community College. Your institution has embraced competency-based education, and programs have worked to align their coursework with industry assessments, so students can earn certification and begin working in their field even before the degree is awarded. This is essential because you are located in rural Appalachia, where industry is declining, and most of your students are from low-income households. You decide to launch the aligned external validation (testing through industry) in two programs: HVAC and Welding, and compare the impact satisfaction to those in programs without external validation (Electrical, Plumbing, and Brick Masonry). You compare program satisfaction without having a baseline and find that students in the programs with external validation are more satisfied. Then you have to ask yourself, is that enough information for you to spread the intervention to the other programs? Is the external validation what is causing the difference in satisfaction?

A common, widely used design is the *before-and-after or pretest/post-test design*. In such a design, you examine the data on some process or outcomes before and after the implementation of some intervention. Depending on the data you have access to, you may collect the data as a part of the PDSA, or the baseline data may already exist. Imagine you are an instructor of an online course in college algebra. Your course set-up is simple, each week there is a video lecture, students have access to the slides, there is a quiz, and a discussion board. You notice after the first major unit test, on algebraic operations, less than 60% of the class is passing, and your analysis of the data provided in your LMS is that most students are not watching the entirety of the lectures. In fact, they are only watching about 15% of the videos—according to the minutes watched per student. You find there is a new feature within your recording software, Panopto, that allows you to embed questions throughout the videos where your students have to answer the question for the video to continue playing and it gives them an additional grade each week.

You implement this change, compare their grades on the unit test (outcome), and compare the minutes watched of the videos (your theory of improvement led you to believe greater engagement with the content would lead to better performance). You find that after the change is implemented, students are watching 85% of the video, and now 68% of the class is passing. You suspect this change may very well be an improvement.

A third design for testing changes is the *time-series design*. There are a number of variations on the time series design, including the before-and-after time series, time series with replication, time series with a control group, and time series with planned grouping (Langley et al., 2009). As the name suggests, time series designs examine data over time and examine only one change at a time. Time series designs in testing changes are very similar to single subject research designs common in special education and counseling. Single-subject designs are described as an "adaptation of a time series design" but they articulate, using letters A for baseline and B for intervention, the adding and removal of a change (Suter, 2012, p. 305). Time series designs rely heavily on the visualization of data over time, and run charts will be used in every type. The before-and-after time series design establishes a baseline and continues to collect the same data after some change. You examine your data to determine if changes in patterns correspond with when the intervention was introduced.

Envision yourself as a science teacher who has just completed some training on Universal Design for Learning (UDL). You have a record of weekly quizzes from the first week of school to now, and you want to implement UDL principles in your lesson plans, particularly with regards to representation, and all the new vocabulary students have to master in science. So, you begin to do so, and you track changes in your weekly quiz grades to see if this has made a difference. This would be a simple time series before-and-after. If you wanted to remove the intervention and then implement it again, which would be an ABAB design, or time series replicated. This design would enable you to determine if, when representation was removed from your lessons your students' quiz grades went back to the baseline, and if the reentry of representation would be as effective as the first time. A time series with a control group would be if you decided to implement to UDL strategy in some class periods but not in others, and compared the classes (this is assuming the classes were similar at the outset). The last time series, with grouping, could be used if you wanted to determine its effectiveness in marketed different groups. For instance, if you had a gifted section and a really low-achieving section, you could see whether the strategy had similar benefits on both groups of students—this would be time series with planned grouping.

When advising doctoral students, I often suggest not to implement more than one intervention at a time, because it becomes difficult to tease out the individual effects. But in practice, multiple initiatives are always being rolled out at once. When you are implementing multiple factors of a change at once, a *factorial design* will yield the most useful information—on the impact of each component and the interaction of the two.

Suppose you are the director of advising at Academic Prowess University, and you have prided yourself on your developmental advising model—designed to help students mature and take responsibility of their plan of study, with support. However, last year, more than 115 students who should have been graduating seniors had to stay an extra semester to take one class. When surveyed, you found that these students were highly unsatisfied with their advising experience and felt they should have known to take the course sooner. After exploring the problem with your team, you have developed two changes in advising: advising approach and type of advisor. You are going to be testing out two different approaches to advising to see if it improves student satisfaction with the process, as well as their knowledge of their degree audit and what they need to take, in order to graduate by their own established deadline. While APU has long embraced developmental advising, you are going to test the effectiveness of prescriptive and intrusive advising. In addition to looking at the approach to advising, you will also look at the types of advisors and whether that makes a difference in student satisfaction and knowledge of what to do next. You have long employed academic advisors who are faculty members who know the programs well. This time, you also want to see the efficacy of professional advisors.

To examine this type of change, you would need to use a factorial design. Because this is a high stakes situation and therefore high-risk, you want to begin on a small scale. You may begin by only looking at the juniors in the Department of Psychology and amongst these juniors, you will divide them randomly among these four different factors as shown below, and then compare their perceptions of their knowledge and their perceptions of their satisfaction at the end of the next semester.

Table 8.1. Advisor Type by Advising Type

		Change 1: Advisor	
		Academic	Professional
Change 2: Approach	Prescriptive	A	B
	Intrusive	C	D

It is important to note in this initiative, you are not looking at how many will stay an extra semester because they did not have the classes they need it to graduate on time. That is a lagging indicator. And you are you will not be able to assess that the outcome immediately, but you will see whether or not they have a better understanding of what they should do and how satisfied they are. You may predict that students feel more satisfied with the intrusive model, but they will actually now have a better handle on what to do with the prescriptive model. As you compare your predictions with your findings, in a subsequent cycle, you may expand to try different conditions, perhaps using freshmen in psychology or juniors in engineering—before you make any decision to adopt the changes.

Approaches to Improvement

This text examines one methodological approach to improvement: improvement science. However, there are multiple frameworks and methodologies people employ for organizational improvement. While the goal of this work is not to be exhaustive, I would be remiss not to acknowledge the various approaches that exist and have found success in education and other sectors. For an in-depth examination of some of these methodologies (and others not discussed here such as positive deviance and deliverology), see the first issue in volume 25 of *Quality Assurance in Education*. Senior Carnegie Fellow, Paul LeMahieu, and an incredible cast of scholars examine seven approaches to improvement and their applicability in education. The section that follows will only introduce you to five: Six Sigma, Lean Six Sigma, Implementation Science, Design-based Implementation Research, and Lesson Study.

Six Sigma

Six Sigma is an improvement methodology that was developed by Motorola in the late 1980s and has quickly gained prominence in manufacturing, retail, and finance. Six Sigma is responsive to the "Voice of Customer (VOC)" and could be described as user-centered (Sokovic, Pavletic, & Pipan, 2010, p. 482). The goal of Six Sigma methodology is to reduce process variation that leads to negative outcomes. In other words, it seeks to minimize the likelihood of errors. The name of the method, "Six Sigma," refers to the measurement of DPMO [defects per million opportunities], and that when a given process is much better than average (highly reliable and stable) its 'sigma' level is equal to 3.4 defects or errors for every million opportunities" (LeMahieu, Nordstrum & Cudney, 2017, p. 92). In essence, this method seeks to have processes in a state of statistical control or stability. In an attempt to control variation, Six Sigma attempts to locate origins in variation by examining six input categories: "materials, methods, man, machine, measurement or the environment" (LeMahieu, Nordstrum & Cudney, 2017, p. 99). Six Sigma has two methodological approaches to problem solving and problem prevention. DMAIC (Define, Measure, Analyze, Improve, and Control) is the Six Sigma cycle for improving process. DMAIC is described as "a rigorous framework of results-oriented project management" (Sokovic et al., 2010, p. 481). Similar to improvement science, the process is iterative in nature. DFSS (Design for Six Sigma) has one primary objective, "design things right the first time," (Sokovic et al., 2010, p. 481). Within DFSS, there are two common approaches to designing new products, processes, or services: DMADV (Define, Measure, Analyze, Design, and Verify) and IDOV (Identify, Design, Optimize, and Validate) (Sokovic et al., 2010, p. 482).

Many people writing about Six Sigma as an improvement methodology draw parallels between the DMAIC and the Plan, Do, Study (Check), Act (PDS[C]A) cycle. Pepper and Spedding contend, "Six Sigma brings structure to process improvement by providing the user with a more detailed outline of Deming's plan-do-check-act cycle by guiding the initiative through a five stage cycle of define-measure-analyze-improve-control (DMAIC)" (p. 142). It is important for improvement scientist to know that people using Six Sigma are employing similar processes with a similar structure to achieve organizational improvement.

Lean & Lean Six Sigma

Lean Six Sigma is an integration of two approaches to improvement, *Lean* and *Six Sigma*. Lean has roots in manufacturing as well, specifically born from the Toyota Production System (Pepper & Spedding, 2009). A lean organization tries to maximize value and trim the waste, but waste is not human capital. The Lean approach identifies seven forms of organizational waste: overproduction, defects, unnecessary inventory, inappropriate processing, excessive transportation, waiting, and unnecessary motion (Pepper & Spedding, 2009, p. 138). The goal of Lean is to identify "value added and non-value adding processes" and of course, eliminate the latter (Pepper & Spedding, 2009, p. 139). Understanding value requires members of Lean organization to be user-centered.

Lean organizations emphasize relationships. LeMahieu, Nordstrum, and Greco explain, "Lean posits that a tightly coupled relationship between providers of and those who receive those services is essential to understanding what value means and for determining how best to deliver it" (2017, p. 75). Value and what processes are considered value-adding is not solely determined by those within the system, but in conjunction with those the system serves.

Lean Six Sigma as an improvement methodology "is used to identify problems, map current states, articulate goals (state targets), suggest interventions (countermeasures), collect data on current system performance and countermeasure implementation and report results" (LeMahieu, Nordstrom & Greco, 2017, p. 79). As it attempts to identify values, one tool it uses in Value Stream Mapping (VSM). VSM is a qualitative analytic tool that "defines the scope of the project by defining the current state and the desired future state of the system" (Pepper & Spedding, 2009, p. 139). Another tool associated with lean processes include 5S which stands for: sort, set in order, shine, standardize, and sustain (Al-Aomar, 2011; Pepper & Spedding, 2009). Again, with roots in manufacturing, this tool is designed to give visual cues that reduce waste and create a clean workplace, reduced set up times, reduced cycle times, and a safer work environment (Al-Aomar, 2011). An additional Lean tool is the A3 report, named after the 11 by 17 paper in which it is printed. The A3 report maps all the components of the improvement process. Chakravorty (2009) argues the "A3 report is an effective tool because it contains not only text, but also pictures, diagrams, and charts, all of which enrich and clarify the data" (p. 7). While there are multiple templates and guidelines, Chakravorty (2009) explains the report consist of two sides. The left side contains the theme (problem[s]), the necessary background information, the current condition (often derived from VSM), and a causal analysis (such as the result from Five Whys technique). The right side of the report contains the target (desired) condition which includes improvement initiatives or countermeasures that will be takes to achieve the condition, the implementation plan, and the follow up plan (and once completed, the actual results).

While some tools in Lean Six Sigma may seem not to be applicable to schools and universities, the principles underlying the improvement can prove to be advantageous to educational systems. Both VSM and A3 reports could be adopted as tools to drive improvements in the educational sector.

Implementation Science

Unlike Six Sigma and Lean Six Sigma, the third improvement methodology was not born from manufacturing—but from healthcare. *Implementation science*, like the name suggests, seeks to understand and alleviate failure and outcome variance due to poor implementation of intervention. Implementation science is attractive to educators who understand policies and programs are often implemented without the expected results. With multiple waves of research of educational policy implementation, involving scholars like Milbrey McLaughlin, Allan Odden, and Meredith Honig, the failure of implementation to produce results with interventions that has long baffled educators.

As the name suggests, the goal of implementation science is to understand the implementation, which also includes the adoption and spread, of programs and interventions (Nordstrum, LeMahieu & Berrena, 2017). The variation implementation science seeks to understand and diminish is variation in outcomes due to implementation. As such, problems of practice in implementation science "have less to do with program effectiveness (what actions might solve some problem) than the adoption and implementation of interventions (thought to be effective) in complex learning environments" (Nordstrum et al., 2017, p. 65). As you saw in the chapter on practical measurement, implementation scientists pay close attention to measures of fidelity and adherence, as they seek to identify and eliminate barriers to implementation (Carroll, Patterson, Wood, Booth, Rick & Balain, 2007).

Implementation science does not have a prescribed method like the PDSA cycle, but there are three "categories of roles" in implementation scientists take on as a part of the process of developing solutions at they are STS, SS, and DS. STS stands for synthesis and translation; this role bridges the research and practice divide by synthesizing "scientific theory and evidence into user friendly interventions" (Nordstrum et al., 2017, p. 66). The second role, SS, signifies support system. This role in implementation science seeks to build the capacity of those implementing the intervention, by building intervention specific capacity or generic capacity. The third and final role for implementation scientists occupy is the DS or delivery support. In this role, the focus is working with the users who will carry out the intervention on the ground.

Implementation science can complement improvement science, as you may conduct PDSAs to determine how to improve the implantation of some change.

Design-Based Implementation Research

Design-based implementation research (DBIR) aims to bridge the divide between research and practice with authentic partnership between scholars and practitioners during the design and implementation phase of educational innovations. Penuel and associates (2011) detail the roots of the name, design-based implementation research, explaining it was chosen because "design thinking figures prominently in it . . . and because research on the implementation of reforms drives iterative improvements to designs" (p. 331).

DBIR is a response to a century old problem in educational innovation and research that started with Taylorism and scientific management. Fisherman and colleagues (2013) explain this history "created a sharp division of labor between those who design innovations and those who implement them" (2013, p. 138). In an attempt to decrease the space between innovation and implementation, DBIR rests on four principles:

1. Persistent problems of practice in education that are persistent problems *from the perspective of multiple stakeholders* [my emphasis]
2. Iterative and collaborative design of programs, changes, or interventions to achieve desired outcomes

3. A commitment to the development of theory about both implementation (processes) and learning (outcomes)
4. A focus on developing organizational capacity to sustain change and improvement in educational systems (Fisherman, Penuel, Allen, Cheng & Sabelli, 2013; LeMahieu, Nordstrum & Potvin, 2017; Penuel, Fisherman, Cheng & Sabelli, 2011; Russell, Jackson, Krumm & Frank, 2013).

As in implementation science, there is no set methodology for engaging in DBIR. In fact, in Russell, Jackson, Krumm, and Frank's (2013) multi-case study of DBIR, they found partnerships using methods from improvement science, design-research, quasi-experiments, and novel methodologies. Improvement science can be embedded in a DBIR initiative.

Lesson Study

The final approach to improvement reviewed in this primer is lesson study. Like DBIR, lesson study does not come from another field, but has a home in the field of education. As the name suggests, *lesson study* is an improvement approach designed to improve instruction by collaboratively studying live lessons. Lesson study was designed for practitioners, not researchers or Six Sigma black belts; this methodology was designed for people engaged in the everyday practice of teaching.

Lesson study traces its origins to Japan as a method of professional development. Like improvement science, it consists of a four part cycle wherein educators: 1) study the curriculum and formulate goals, 2) develop a plan (design a lesson that they believe will help them achieve the goal), 3) they conduct research (implement and study the lesson in practice), and 4) they reflect on what has happened (Lewis, Perry & Murata, 2006). Perry and Lewis (2008) explain in steps three and four that during implementation, teachers involved:

> Conduct the lesson in a classroom, with one team member teaching and others gathering evidence on student learning and development; reflect on and discuss the evidence gathered during the

lesson, using it to improve the lesson, the unit, and instruction more generally; and if desired, teach, observe, and improve the lesson again in one or more additional classrooms. (p. 366)

In many ways, its iterative nature is similar to that of improvement science.

Lesson study has experienced success improving instruction in the United States classrooms. As a method, it is described as "easy to learn but difficult to master" (Chokshi & Fernandez, 2004, p. 524). Like all improvement methodologies, "like a map, lesson study is a tool for going somewhere. But important questions to keep in mind are where we want to go, how we want to get there, and what signposts we will use along the way" (Chokshi & Fernandez, 2004, p. 524). These questions sound similar to, "What am I trying to address?" "What change might I introduce?" and "Why, and how, will I know that change is an improvement?" For those working specifically to improve instruction, lesson study may be an advantageous improvement approach.

Improvement Methodologies and the PDSA

There are many approaches to improvement and improvement research in education. The purpose here is exposure, not to elevate one over the other. Each of these approaches has merit and can be beneficial to improving opportunities to learn for students. What makes improvement science advantageous and a nice entry point for practitioners is its adaptability to all types of problems. The PDSA cycle can focus on implementation or the testing of a new innovation. It can be used to explore processes or document the impact on outcomes.

The PDSA cycle is *the* method in improvement science. It is essential that you do not claim to use improvement science if you are deviating greatly from the method. Each phase, plan-do-study-and act, adds to your knowledge and understanding of how to improve; shortchanging any of them shortchanges the entire process. Improvement science is designed to be iterative, small-scale tests of change. As you engage in the PDSA cycle, you cannot neglect the other principles—you must remain user centered; you must continue to monitor variation; you must observe how change takes place in the larger system; you must rely on your practical measures. This method combines theory and science with persistence, and it can drive improvement in educational organizations if employed as designed.

Disciplined inquiry will lead you to know whether your change idea has merit. In general, to estimate the impact of a change, you probably do not want to implement more than one or two changes at a time. After you find change idea works, you may adopt it, or expand it to another part of the organization. Yet, as you generated change ideas, you generated many ideas that have yet to be evaluated. How long will it take you to test all of those ideas to determine which is the most effective or what is the most effective combinations? Weeks? Months? Years?

Accelerating change, and testing multiple change ideas simultaneously, is where the power of networks lies. The final improvement principle, explored in chapter 9, illustrates how to accelerate improvement by working in concert with others on the same problem of practice.

Key Terms

- **Before-and-After/Pre-test-Post-testdesign**—The before-and-after or pre-test-post-test design is one of multiple research designs that can be employed within a PDSA cycle. It establishes a baseline (pre-test), employs a change, and then compares the outcomes after the change with the baseline.
- **Charter**—A charter is a guiding document that outlines the goals, theory, measurement, and methods of an improvement initiative.
- **Design team**—Improvement science is not a personal project; it is collaborative in nature. To design impactful changes, practitioners must rely on the expertise of a wide array of stakeholders. A design team is a team of stakeholders who possess the knowledge to understand (define) problems and design (develop) solutions within an organization.

- **Design-based implementation research**—DBIR is an improvement methodology that seeks to address persistent problems of practice by bridging the divide between scholars and practitioners to decrease the distance between innovation and implementation. It is guided by four principles and has no prescribed methodology. Improvement science can be the methodological approach employed in DBIR.
- **Factorial design**—A factorial design is one of multiple research designs that can be employed during PDSA cycles. A factorial design is appropriate when more than one change is being assessed at a time. A factorial design helps practitioners estimate individual effects of each change as well as interaction effects.
- **Implementation science**—Implementation science is an improvement methodology that seeks to understand variance in program outcomes due to implementation.
- **Implementation team**—An implementation team is a team of stakeholders within an organization tasked with implementing a change (intervention, new process, new technology) as a part of the improvement science process.
- **Iterative cycles**—Iterative cycles are one of the hallmarks of improvement science process. They illustrate the continuousness of continuous improvement, as each cycle is informed by the previous cycle.
- **Lean Six Sigma**—Lean Six Sigma is an integration of two improvement methodologies, Lean, which focuses on a reduction of waste, and Six Sigma, which focuses on a reduction in process variation.
- **Lesson study**—Lesson study is an improvement methodology designed to improve instruction. The collaborative method, designed for teachers, consists of a four-step cycle that begins with studying curricula and formulating goals, developing a plan (lesson) that will achieve the goals, studying the lesson (as implemented in a real classroom), and then reflecting on the process. Educators can revise and reteach the lesson as needed.
- **Model for Improvement**—The Model for Improvement (MFI) is advanced in the text, *The Improvement Guide*. The MFI is the interplay of the three essential improvement science questions (What am I trying to accomplish? How will I know if a change

is an improvement? What change might I introduce and why?) and the PDSA methodology.

- **Observational design**—An observational design is one of multiple research designs that can be employed within the PDSA cycle. In this design, you compare two groups after employing a change or intervention with one group to see how they differ. It is similar to a quasi-experiment.

- **Participant observer**—In ethnographic or observational research, a participant observer is one who has dual roles; they are involved with the phenomenon under investigation as well as an investigator. They must pay close attention to what is happening to accurately capture events and processes, and must try to the extent possible to document their role and influence on what transpires. They use fieldnotes (journals, maps, video diaries, etc.) to try to accurately capture with the least amount of bias.

- **PDCA/FOCUS PDCA**—The PDCA is a continuous improvement cycle—Plan-Do-Check and Act that originates in Japan. The distinction between the PDSA and the PDCA cycle is that PDCAs look more narrowly at faults within system processes, whereas the PDSA had a broader application (processes, products, programs, etc.). The FOCUS PDCA is similar to the *Model for Improvement*, as it has five steps preceding the PDCA methodology, as the three essential questions lead into the PDSA cycle.

- **PDSA cycle**—The Plan Do Study Act cycle is the signature improvement science methodology. It combines deductive and inductive forms of inquiry in iterative cycles to improve problems of practice. It has four distinct phases, from which its name is derived, planning, doing, studying, and acting.

- **Six Sigma**—Six Sigma is an improvement methodology that seeks to reduce process variation that leads to negative outcomes.

- **Small-scale tests**—Small-scale tests are another hallmark of improvement science. Imbedded in this strategy is the desire to ensure a change/intervention is efficacious before implementing on a large scale. Furthermore, with each test, practitioners learn more about the change and the process of implementation—and that information can inform efforts to spread.

- **Time series design**—A time series design in one of multiple research designs that can be employed within a PDSA framework. Similar to single-subject research, it follows the data on outcomes or processes over time. It examines the variation during the introduction of an intervention and the removal of that intervention.

Questions for Improving with Equity in Mind: Who Is Involved? Who Is Impacted?

- Will the aim of my improvement initiative lead to increased opportunities to learn for all students? Traditionally underserved students?
- Do my design team and implementation team reflect the diversity of thought needed to develop the best improvements?
  - Whose voice or presence is missing on my teams that should be reflected?
- Is my charter written in a way that makes it accessible to all stakeholders involved with the improvement? All stakeholders in the organization?
- Is my documentation in the "Do" phase reflective of all stakeholders' experiences?
  - Whose experiences are missing?
- Whose perspective and suggestions were considered in deciding next steps in the "Act" phase?
  - Whose perspectives and suggestions were overlooked? Ignored?

References

Al-Aomar, R. A. (2011). Applying 5S LEAN technology: An infrastructure for continuous process improvement. *World Academy of Science, Engineering and Technology*, *59*, 2014–2019.

Batalden, P. B., & Stoltz, P. K. (1995). Quality management and continual improvement of health care: A framework. *Journal of Continuing Education in the Health Professions*, *15*(3), 146–164.

Carroll, C., Patterson, M., Wood, S., Booth, A., Rick, J., & Balain, S. (2007). A conceptual framework for implementation fidelity. *Implementation Science, 2*(1), 40.

Chakravorty, S. S. (2009). Process improvement: using Toyota's A3 reports. *Quality Management Journal, 16*(4), 7–26.

Chokshi, S., & Fernandez, C. (2004). Challenges to importing Japanese lesson study: Concerns, misconceptions, and nuances. *Phi Delta Kappan, 85*(7), 520–525.

Deming, W. E. (2000/1986). *Out of the crisis.* Cambridge, MA: MIT Press.

Deming, W. E. (2000/1994). *The new economics for industry, government, education.* Cambridge, MA: MIT Press.

Fishman, B. J., Penuel, W. R., Allen, A. R., Cheng, B. H., & Sabelli, N. O. R. A. (2013). Design-based implementation research: An emerging model for transforming the relationship of research and practice. *National Society for the Study of Education, 112*(2), 136–156.

Langley, G. J., Moen, R. D., Nolan, K. M., Nolan, T. W., Norman, C. L., & Provost, L. P. (2009). *The improvement guide: A practical approach to enhancing organizational performance.* Hoboken, NJ: John Wiley & Sons.

LeMahieu, P. G., Nordstrum, L. E., & Cudney, E. A. (2017). Six Sigma in education. *Quality Assurance in Education, 25*(1), 91–108.

LeMahieu, P. G., Nordstrum, L. E., & Greco, P. (2017). Lean for education. *Quality Assurance in Education, 25*(1), 74–90.

LeMahieu, P. G., Nordstrum, L. E., & Potvin, A. S. (2017). Design-based implementation research. *Quality Assurance in Education. 25*(1) p.26-42.

Lewis, C., Perry, R., & Murata, A. (2006). How should research contribute to instructional improvement? The case of lesson study. *Educational Researcher, 35*(3), 3–14.

Moen, R., & Norman, C. (2006). *Evolution of the PDCA cycle.* http://citeseerx.ist.psu.edu/viewdoc/download?doi=10.1.1.470.5465&rep=rep1&type=pdf. Accessed October 7, 2019.

Nordstrum, L. E., LeMahieu, P. G., & Berrena, E. (2017). Implementation science: Understanding and finding solutions to variation in program implementation. *Quality Assurance in Education, 25*(1), 58–73.

Penuel, W. R., Fishman, B. J., Haugan Cheng, B., & Sabelli, N. (2011). Organizing research and development at the intersection of learning, implementation, and design. *Educational Researcher, 40*(7), 331–337.

Pepper, M. P., & Spedding, T. A. (2010). The evolution of lean six sigma. *International Journal of Quality & Reliability Management, 27*(2), 138–155.

Perry, R. R., & Lewis, C. C. (2009). What is successful adaptation of lesson study in the US? *Journal of Educational Change, 10*(4), 365–391.

Russell, J. L., Jackson, K., Krumm, A. E., & Frank, K. A. (2013). Theories and research methodologies for design-based implementation research: Examples from four cases. *Yearbook of the National Society for the Study of Education, 112*(2), 157–191.

Shewhart, W. A., & Deming, W. E. (1986). *Statistical method from the viewpoint of quality control.* North Chelmsford, Massachusetts: Courier Corporation.

Sokovic, M., Pavletic, D., & Pipan, K. K. (2010). Quality improvement methodologies–PDCA cycle, RADAR matrix, DMAIC and DFSS. *Journal of Achievements in Materials and Manufacturing Engineering, 43*(1), 476–483.

Speroff, T., & O'Connor, G. T. (2004). Study designs for PDSA quality improvement research. *Quality Management in Healthcare, 13*(1), 17–32.

Suter, W. N. (2011). *Introduction to educational research: A critical thinking approach.* Thousand Oaks, CA: Sage.

Taylor, M. J., McNicholas, C., Nicolay, C., Darzi, A., Bell, D., & Reed, J. E. (2014). Systematic review of the application of the plan–do–study–act method to improve quality in healthcare. *BMJ Quality and Safety, 23*(4), 290–298.

CHAPTER NINE

Accelerating Improvement with Networks

Many hands make light work.
—Haya (Tanzanian) proverb

Throughout this primer, I have argued improvement science is a methodological framework that is undergirded by foundational principles that guide scholar-practitioners to define problems, understand how the system produces the problems, identify changes to rectify the problems, test the efficacy of those changes, and spread the changes (if the change is indeed an improvement). The tools presented up until this point are designed to aid teams within organizations or the same system to tackle problems of practice that arise in their organization. However, in the field of education, problems of practice tend to be common, despite contexts being unique. Rural schools across the country face the problem of their students having connectivity issues at home, predominately White colleges and universities across the country are wrestling how to create inclusive campus cultures, community colleges across the country are trying to how best to serve incoming students who were employed in industries that are disappearing. We have common problems in unique contexts.

If you choose not to read this chapter, you have some good insights on how to improve a problem of practice within your organization, one change idea at a time. Or in an organization large enough with multiple teams, you may be able to conduct PDSAs on different things simultaneously. But the truth is, once you have created that theory of improvement, and you have developed those change ideas, there are usually more changes than there is manpower to test them. So, as you study and refine one, there are another 30 waiting for the same level of study and refinement. But who has the time? Chances are your job title is not improvement science specialist and your sole job is not to test the efficacy of changes. There are competing priorities. So, how do we accelerate change?

In this chapter, we will explore the power of networks as a mechanism for accelerating improvement. I will introduce you to the phenomena of networks and Network Improvement Communities; I will explore the multiple levels at which organizational learning can take place; I will give an overview of the guidance in the field about creating networks, and I will encourage readers to build networks with an expressed commitment to advancing equity.

The Power of Networks

The final principle of improvement science, as articulated by Bryk, Gomez, Grunow, and LeMahieu (2015), is to accelerate the learning through the use of networks. A network can be defined as, "an interconnected group of people; an organization; *spec.* a group of people having certain connections . . . which may be exploited to gain preferment, information, etc., esp. for professional advantage" ("network," 2019). The connotation of "exploit" is usually negative, but networks in improvement science enable all members to gain information for professional (or organizational) advantage. When there are multiple organizations focusing on the same problem of practice, it becomes like the old cliché—together, everyone achieves more—the network becomes a team.

Bryk and associates advance the term *Network Improvement Communities*, or *NICs*, to describe networks collectively working on a singular aim. NICs have four defining features:

1. NICs are focused on a singular aim.
2. NICs are guided by a deep understanding of the problem and the system that produces it. They also share a theory of improvement.
3. NICs use improvement science, or improvement research, to understand the efficacy of interventions to address the problem.
4. NICs organize to spread knowledge of effective interventions throughout the field and their own organizations. (Bryk et al., 2015; Dolle, Gomez, Russell & Bryk, 2013; Russell, Bryk, Dolle, Gomez & LeMahieu, 2017)

In listing the requirements above, Russel et al. (2017) highlighted some key words to describe NICS: focused, guided, disciplined (with regard to inquiry), and coordinated. NICs exploit information in order to improve. While networks are common in education, all networks are not NICs. In fact, Bryk and associates (2015) explain:

> Learning communities, communities of practice, and some forms of researcher-practitioner partnerships often describe their efforts as "learning together." Typically, these communities are convened around some common interest coupled with social affinity. Participants may engage in compelling discussion about a common problem and share reflections about things they have tried. However, *they do not commit to achieving a specific improvement nor measure progress toward it* [my emphasis]. (p. 150)

Gomez and collaborators (2016) distinguish between types of networks, denoting them as sharing networks or execution networks. Communities of practice are considered sharing networks; whereas NICs are execution networks. Every network is not in an NIC.

Accelerating Improvement

You may be wondering how networks accelerate improvement. It is more than a simple understanding of "two heads are better than one," but practically, organizations tackling the same problem simultaneously can generate different amounts of information about how to address the problem of practice in a variety of contexts, under a variety of different conditions. The work of Douglas Englebart serves as the basis of the improvement science understanding of the power of networks (Bryk et al., 2015). If you simply employ what has been discussed in the previous chapters in your own organization, you would develop knowledge on two levels, the A level, or individual level, and the B level—the organization level. As depicted below, and adapted from the model in *Learning to Improve*, networks allow you to generate C-level knowledge.

Figure 9.1. Levels of Learning

When you think about a personal problem of practice and develop a theory of improvement, examine all the potential change ideas and concept that results from your analysis of the problem and understanding of the system. As you see the system, you may recognize there is no one silver bullet, but it will take a multitiered approach to solving your problem of practice. Suppose you are the director of distance education and online learning at City State College (CSC) and retention in your online courses is dismal. You have a withdrawal rate of nearly 50%, and Ds and Fs at about 20%. Imagine your team created the driver diagram pictured in 6.5 (as well as below in 9.2) about improving retention in online classes.

Figure 9.2. Driver Diagram

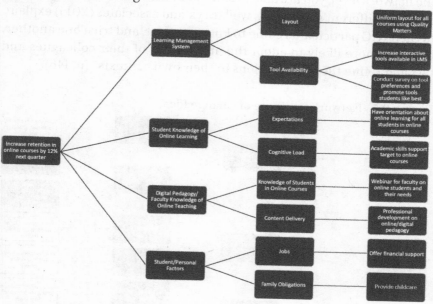

Immediately, you see there are multiple change ideas that could lead to improvement. Bryk and colleagues (2015) elucidate the possibility that exists within networks: "By parsing a very large problem into many discrete subtasks, it eases entry for individual participation ... an individual NIC member can work on just a single change idea imbedded in the structure of a much larger improvement effort" (p. 146). This means if CSC was a part of a network on online student retention, different institutions within the network could take on the different change ideas simultaneously. If you had a network of nine institutions, two institutions could work on designing courses using the Quality Matters guidelines, three may focus on designing an orientation for online students, two may focus on developing academic skills support to online students, and two may focus on a developing a webinar for faculty on online teaching. In developing these changes, they could also share resources, and could even make the same webinar available at both institutions.

Collectively, your network has covered nearly half of your change ideas, and has multiple institutions working on each one. Therefore, at the network level, you are able to learn about the nuances of implementation in different contexts as well. Bryk and associates (2015) explain, "When NIC participants come to know, respect, and trust one another, they are more likely to adopt the innovations of their colleagues and test and refine these innovations in their own contexts" (p. 146).

Figure 9.3. Network Coverage of Change Ideas

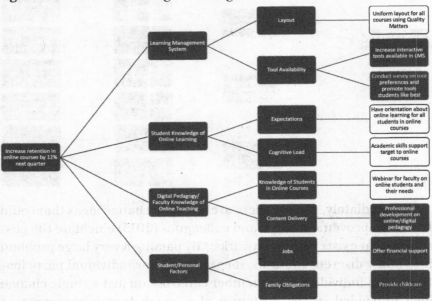

Now you can decide based on the results at your peer institutions in the NIC whether it is advantageous for CSC to adopt the other change ideas that have been tested and found effective. After studying these four, the network may move on to adding testing additional change ideas as well.

Developing NICs

While NICs are wonderful, developing an NIC is no small task. Russell and colleagues (2017) have developed a framework around five domains that "they hypothesize are critical to initiate a viable network improvement community" (p. 13). They operationalize as viable a network that is both sustainable and achieves its aim. The five domains are as follows:

- Developing a theory of practice improvement
- Using improvement research methods
- Developing a measurement and analytics infrastructure
- Leading, organizing, and operating the network
- And developing culture, norms, and identity for the network (Russell et al., 2017)

Russell and associates (2017) depict this framework in concentric circles and explain the first three domains are the technical core.

Figure 9.4. Framework for Initiating Networked Improvement Communities

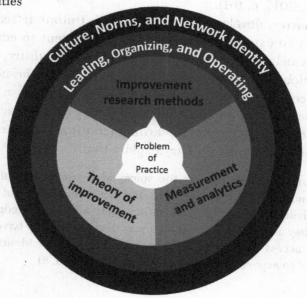

A central aim and shared problem of practice is the foundation of the NIC. However, having a shared theory about how to address this problem is essential, too. If you see the system one way and another organization sees the driving factors in the system in a completely different way, you will be headed in different directions and not building knowledge on the same theory. A common language, a common goal, and a common understanding of the system that produces the results are necessary for the network to be functional.

Bryk et al. (2015) suggest the employment of a *Network Initiation Team* in the early phases of development of an NIC. This team does some of the heavy lifting in the beginning by defining the aim, studying the system, and taking an initial stab at creating the theory of improvement. With that working theory, they embrace a "guiding spirit" that says the theory is "possible wrong and definitely incomplete" (2015, p. 163). This guiding stance illustrates a position of humility and acknowledges they may learn things and need to revise the theory. This team develops a charter for the NIC. This document, while living and revisable, allows "informed participation," meaning people join who join the NIC already understand the aim and the theory are going to inform improvement efforts (Bryk et al., 2015, p. 161).

The charter, developed by the Network Initiation Team, is an opportunity to express the network's commitment to equity. The document can lay the foundation for the network's culture, or shared values (which is depicted in the outer ring). While the network is expressly committed to continuous improvement—as a Network *Improvement* Community, Fullan and Malloy (2019) discuss there is often a disconnect between learning (continuous improvement) culture and equity culture. They explain that:

> A culture of equity centers the voices and experiences of those most underserved in all decisions. Further, the dynamic of power and privilege are not ignored; rather, they are acknowledged for what they are, which is the unjust way that people may have more or less access to opportunities based solely on their identifies as opposed to expertise. (Fullan & Malloy, 2019, para. 8)

In education, we have made more progress in embracing organizational learning cultures than equity ones. As the initiation team defines the aim as well as norms for participation, they should be asking *who is involved* with our definition of what is important and *who will be impacted* when our aims are achieved. Furthermore, they even need to think about the makeup of the team. While networks have to consider which prospective members have the capacity to be a part of the network, there may be other organizations or institutions with less capacity or resources that have insight to help articulate aims and theories of improvement. It is essential that networks discover high-leverage changes that work in under resourced organizations.

A second component of the technical core is a commitment to using improvement research methods, such as the PDSA cycles discussed in the previous chapter. Russell et al. (2017) explain that in their experience, during early phases of NIC formation, it is essential to take time to build capacity amount network leaders and participants to engage in this form of inquiry. Hand in hand with the disciplined inquiry is the analytic and measurement infrastructure. Scholars explain that the network's:

> Improvement activity is anchored in a measurement and analytics infrastructure that enables the NIC to establish whether specific changes introduced into local systems are generating the immediate process results expected and whether these in turn, link to key drivers and the ultimate outcomes that the NIC seeks. (Russell et al., 2017, p. 19)

LeMahieu and colleagues suggest this analytic infrastructure contains a "family of measures" that explicitly support the logic of assessing some change intervention . . . Such a family of measures includes here components of paralleling the logic of improvement: process measures, outcome measures and balancing measures" (2017, p. 18). A network works best when its members are speaking the same language, and that includes measures that operationalize the theory of improvement. The shared theory, shared method, and shared measures make up the technical core.

But for a sustainable NIC, you need more than the technical core, and this is where you move into the two outer rings of the framework. Leadership, organization, and operation are critical to the NIC's success. Networks are voluntary organizations, so leadership has to drive membership with a commitment to a common vision. The network initiation team must also think about who is needed in the network's membership and what are the criteria for membership. In our example above, to see the success of these initiatives, you need fellow members who have online programs. You also need members who have the capacity to carry out the changes and test them. The initiation team has to think about methods of communication (how often, what medium) through the network—and how the network will run with no true hierarchy in leadership. Sometimes there are hub organizations, and the Carnegie Foundation for the Advancement for Teaching has served as a hub for several networks. In other cases, members must determine where the hub of the network will be, and if that hub will shift from one member institution to another over time. The initiation team may want to draft governing documents for the NIC, so that expectations will be clear when members join.

The final ring in the framework, Russell and associates articulate the importance of shared narratives in the initial developments of a NIC's culture, norms, and identity. Statements about what the NIC is committed to, and what it values, allow organizations to assess their own against what is stated and determined fit.

NICs in Practice

It is important for readers to know that while this chapter includes a fictional example, NICs have been successful in practice. Gomez and associates (2016) explain it is best to employ NICs when dealing with "wicked" problems, which have "unique solutions that evolve through iterative refinement" and are "complex with multiple causes" and do not have a straightforward answer (2016, p. 2016). Many problems in education, especially those related to equity and opportunity, are wicked problems. Several NICs have taken on difficult problems with success. One of the most written about is the Community College Pathways also known as the Carnegie Math Pathways (Dolle et al., 2013; Gomez et al., 2016; LeMahieu et al., 2017; Russell et al., 2017). This NIC examined the decreasing amount of time students spend in developmental math, so they could more quickly get to college level mathematics, with two paths: Statway and Quantway. The research on the impact of the changes is more than promising, with Statway showing positive effects regardless of level of placement, gender, and ethnicity (Yamada, 2014; Yamada & Bryk, 2016). Other NICs working on wicked problems include the Mathematics Teacher Education Partnership (MTEP) designed to secure secondary mathematics teachers (Gomez et al., 2016) and the Beginning Teacher Effectiveness Network designed to give teachers prompt feedback to guide their development (Russell et al., 2017).

A Perfect Time for NICs in K-12 Education

While NICs are appropriate at all levels and sectors of education, the current nature of education reform lends itself to the use of this strategy. School improvement networks are touted as "among the most important educational innovations in the last decade" (Glazer & Peurach, 2012, p. 677). As hub organizations, school improvement networks such as New Tech Network and Big Picture Learning have the capacity to support not only their missions, but NICs as well. Peurach and associates argue in light of this development in school reform, educators must "require that school improvement networks learn to learn" (2016, p. 614).

The Need for NICs

Education is plagued with wicked problems and we can get to sustainable, transformative solutions faster together. As a scholar-practitioner, you can use the first five principles of improvement science in your own organization and see growth and change. But if you want to share your knowledge and accelerate improvement by learning from those facing similar problems, NICs are the way to go. This chapter is not designed to give any illusions of ease in the creation of NICs, but to show the extraordinary power they can possess for improving education once they are established. As Gomez and associates (2016) explain, this is what the complexity requires of us.

Key Terms

- **Network Improvement Community**—An NIC community is an execution network (as opposed to a sharing network), designed to address a particular aim. The networks collaboratively address problems of practice in an effort to accelerate improvement.
- **Network Initiation Team**—A network initiation team is a group committed to establishing a network improvement community. The team does some of the initial work of the NIC such as defining the problem, studying the system, and outlining the theory of improvement. They may also create guiding documents such as a network charter that outlines requirements for membership.

Questions for Improvement with Equity in Mind: Who Is Involved? Who Is Impacted?

- Will achieving our network aim increase opportunities to learn for all students?
  - For traditionally underserved students?
- Do our network documents, such as the charter, reflect a commitment to equity and educational justice?
- Who may benefit from what we're learning in our NIC but does not have the capacity to commit to being a part of the network?
  - How can we share what we know with them?
  - How can they share what they know with us?

References

Bryk, A. S., Gomez, L. M., Grunow, A., & LeMahieu, P. G. (2015). *Learning to improve: How America's schools can get better at getting better.* Cambridge, MA: Harvard Education Press.

Dolle, J. R., Gomez, L. M., Russell, J. L., & Bryk, A. S. (2013). More than a network: Building professional communities for educational improvement. *National Society for the Study of Education Yearbook, 112*(2), 443–463.

Fullan, M., & Malloy, J. (24 Nov 2019). Why is the relationship between 'learning culture' and 'equity culture' so lopsided? *Peter Dewitt's Finding Common Ground [Education Week's Blog].* Retrieved from: http://blogs.edweek.org/edweek/finding_common_ground/2019/11/why_is_the_relationship_between_learning_culture_and_equity_culture_so_lopsided.html

Glazer, J. L., & Peurach, D. J. (2012). School improvement networks as a strategy for large-scale education reform: The role of educational environments. *Educational Policy, 27*(4), 676–710. http://dx.doi.org/10.1177/0895904811429283

Glazer, J. L., & Peurach, D. J. (2013). School improvement networks as a strategy for large-scale education reform: The role of educational environments. *Educational Policy, 27*(4), 676–710.

Gomez, L. M., Russell, J. L., Bryk, A. S., LeMahieu, P. G., & Mejia, E. M. (2016). The right network for the right problem. *Phi Delta Kappan, 98*(3), 8–15.

LeMahieu, P. G., Grunow, A., Baker, L., Nordstrum, L. E., & Gomez, L. M. (2017). Networked improvement communities: The discipline of improvement science meets the power of networks. *Quality Assurance in Education, 25*(1), 5–25.

Network. (2019). Def. 5b. In *Oxford English Dictionary.* Retrieved from https://www.oed.com/

Peurach, D. J., Glazer, J. L., & Winchell Lenhoff, S. (2016). The developmental evaluation of school improvement networks. *Educational Policy, 30*(4), 606–648.

Russell, J. L., Bryk, A. S., Dolle, J., Gomez, L. M., LeMahieu, P., & Grunow, A. (2017). A framework for the initiation of networked improvement communities. *Teachers College Record, 119*(7), 1–36.

Yamada, H. (2014). Community College Pathways' Program Success: Assessing the First Two Years' Effectiveness of Statway®. *Carnegie Foundation for the Advancement of Teaching*. Retrieved from: https://www.carnegiefoundation.org/wp-content/uploads/2014/11/CCP_Statway_Success_Nov_2014.pdf

Yamada, H., & Bryk, A. S. (2016). Assessing the first two years' effectiveness of Statway®: A multilevel model with propensity score matching. *Community College Review, 44*(3), 179–204.

CHAPTER TEN

Improvement Science in Education

Education can't save us. We have to save education.
—Bettina Love

Difficult takes a day. Impossible takes a week.
—Jay Z

Our educational system is broken. Despite all we know about teaching and learning, our educational system continues to advantage some while relegating others. Deficit ideology pervades the minds of educators at all levels, and practices and policies stemming from such understandings continue to reproduce inequalities within our society. Students of color, particularly indigenous, Black, and Latinx students, continue to be overrepresented in special education and underrepresented in gifted programs. These underserved populations, as well as LGBTQ and poor students, are also more likely to be the recipients of punitive discipline policies. The achievement disparity between White, middle-class students and their peers (students of color and non-affluent Whites) reflects the inequity in opportunity. Education was once believed to be a force for economic mobility; now we see greater access to higher education is often also leading to greater debt (sometimes absent degree attainment).

As Love is quoted above, in its current form, education will not save us. Yet, we have to be audacious enough to believe we can save education. No matter how bleak or how big, how wicked or how complex the problem, we have to have faith that we have the knowledge, the power, the tools, and the capacity to tackle it. But first, we must have the will. We must name the problem, and we must see the system.

As critical pragmatists and scholar-practitioners, we must also recognize that continuous improvement, alone, will not save us either. Educators have been engaged in continuous improvement efforts for decades, and we have only become more efficient in our stratification. We have adopted and adapted one innovation after the next, and sometimes when the innovation failed, we found fault in the students we serve, rather than our implementation or improper selection. Time and time again, we have failed to be user-centered; but in our own arrogance, we have tried to prescribe what is best for people without consulting them. We must do better.

There is no doubt that our nation's educational institutions need to improve. Furthermore, there is no doubt that practitioners and researchers alike have long been committed to improvement. The purpose of this text, and this critique, is not to diminish or overlook their efforts, but to build upon them. Improvement science is about learning to improve. It is *literally* the science of improvement. And within improvement science, we define what it means to improve. We can define improvement in terms of equity—if we so choose. Improvement science is a method, with an array of tools, that practitioners can latch on to and apply to a variety of problems of practice, and yield real results—not only change, but improvement.

The problems of practice we face in the field of education, broadly defined, are wicked. They are wicked because the systems that produce them are complex systems, and solutions are not linear and straightforward. They are also wicked in the traditional sense of the word, morally bankrupt, dangerous, and harmful. Addressing educational disparities, in inputs and outputs, requires iterative cycles. The iterativeness advanced here is not an endorsement of slow, incremental change—that has historically been a signifier of no change. To the contrary, the small rapid tests of change, and the adjustments to programs and interventions as a result of these tests, should accelerate improvement. Improvement science is not asking you to wait, but asking instead that you rev up your efforts and get results sooner rather than later. Our students do not have time for us to be slow about improving.

This short text on the science of improvement had two primary aims: to introduce practitioners to, or build upon, practitioners' knowledge of improvement science and to illustrate the applicability of improvement science to issues of equity and justice. Improvement without equity results in efficient reproduction of the status quo. Throughout this primer, at the end of each chapter on the principles and practices of improvement science (chapters 3 through 9), I have shared questions for you to ask yourself (and your team) throughout the process to see if you are improving with equity in mind. In order to improve with equity in mind, you have to think about *who is involved* in the improvement (whose voices have been considered in the definition of the problem and the design of the solution) and *who is impacted* by the improvement. While most examples in this text have been student-centered, all improvement initiatives will not focus on student outcomes. Even as you proceed with operational improvements, you have to continue to ask who benefits from different efficiencies: Is it the administrators at the top? Will people at the bottom lose hours or shifts as a result of this change? Thinking critically about involvement and impact at all stages of the cycle will help avoid negative, unintended consequences.

After reading this book, I hope you take with you: the essential improvement science questions, the foundational questions for improving with equity, the principles of improvement science, the methodology (PDSA cycle), and an appreciation of the power and potential held in networks. The essential improvement science questions are as follows:

- What is the exact problem I'm trying to solve? OR What am I trying to accomplish?
- How will I know a change is an improvement?
- What change might I introduce and why?

Throughout the literature, you may find these questions phrased a bit differently, but the gist is the same. What is the aim, what are the measures, and what is the change? The foundational questions for improving with equity, that must be revisited at all stages of the improvement process are:

- Who is involved?
- Who is impacted?

The six principles of improvement science are as follows:

1. Be user-centered and problem specific.
2. Pay close attention to variation.
3. Recognize the system producing the results.
4. Use practical measures because you cannot improve what you cannot measure.
5. Use disciplined inquiry to drive improvement.
6. Accelerate improvement with networks.

Some of these principles had tools aligned with them to guide your team's improvement initiates.

The tools explored in this primer are summarized here:

Figure 10.1. *Tools Aligned with Improvement Science Principles*

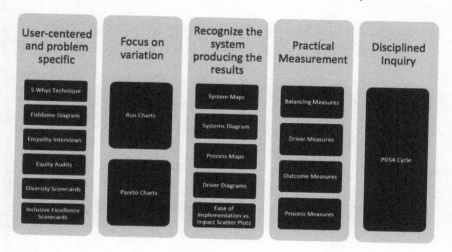

Our students (children and adults) cannot afford for us to do more of the same. Haphazard adoption of the trending educational innovations, ineffective implementation, and premature abandonment are failing to address gaps in educational opportunities. In our current system, we see that the very institutions designed to cultivate individuals' potential is actually stifling it. I hope, in the previous pages, you have seen the practicality and wide applicability of improvement science to tackle problems of practice in your organization. As we deal with a complex system that produces educational inequalities, it will take methods that can handle the complexity to understand how to dismantle that system. Remember the central law of improvement: *Every system is perfectly designed to get the results it gets.* It is time for us to design better systems. Fundamental change that alters system performance (and changes our normal) is what our students deserve, *and* it is the moral imperative of educators in this time.

EPILOGUE

Why Does a Black Girl Endorse Improvement Science?

I believe I'll run on and see what the end is gonna be.
—Black Gospel Music

Some of you may pick up this book and say, "Brandi Hinnant-Crawford? Who is she? Who is she to be writing about improving science?" And the truth is, I am no Tony Bryk. I am no W. E. Deming. I have not spent my career studying organizational improvement; some may say that my career is just beginning. But I am a critical pragmatist. And I want to take a moment to be explicit about my personal axiology and the positionality that led me to write this primer.

In education, we often talk about our positionality. And with social science research, particularly of a qualitative variety, we are asked to be explicit about our positionality because where we sit in the world informs our worldview. We all have multiple identity markers that situate our life experiences. I am a Black, heterosexual, cisgender, Christian woman from eastern North Carolina. I am the divorced, single mother of fraternal twins, Elizabeth Freedom and Elijah Justice Crawford. I am the daughter of an educator who taught in Title I schools her entire career, serving poor Black children. I went to schools that served poor Black children for elementary and secondary schools. I was a high school English teacher in the same high school I graduated from. I lived the first half of my life in highly segregated schools. In my graduating class of over 200, there were only two White students, and I graduated in 2002.

Yet, I am my mother's daughter. I heard the discourse about children who went to school "in the city," but I watched my mother's commitment. She stayed at her elementary through state takeovers and being run by educational management organizations, and for her, it was always about the children. She loved the children and saw potential where others saw a lost cause. I pursued education as a field because I believed in the transformative power that liberatory education could have. There was a time, like Horace Mann, I believed education could be the great equalizer. Now, I have come to view the system we have created as the great stratifier. So how does that lead me to writing a primer on improving science?

When I was a girl, I grew up wanting to change the world. As a small child, I wanted to be the first Black female president. In undergrad, I said I wanted to be the US Secretary of Education. As I have gotten older, I believe the power to make a difference is not in the hands of those at the top and in ostensible positions of power, but the true power lies in the hands of those on the ground. I have witnessed flawed implementation of one policy after another. It was my frustration with what I was witnessing that led me to pursue a master's in urban education policy so I could understand and try to manipulate the political system to work in favor of those in the margins. Then I realized even good policy can have negative consequences when not implemented as intended. I continued on my quest to find "what works." And I have yet to find the silver bullet.

Since reading *In Search of Our Mothers' Garden*, I have always identified with Alice Walker's (1983) definition of womanist. Portions of it describe me to a *T*:

> Wanting to know more and in greater depth than is considered "good" for one. Interested in grown up doings. Acting grown up. Being grown up. Interchangeable with another black folk expression: "You trying to be grown." Responsible. In charge. *Serious.* Loves music. Loves dance. Loves the moon. *Loves* the Spirit. Loves

love and food and roundness. Loves struggle. *Loves* the Folk. Loves herself. *Regardless.* (xi–xii)

So, I heard some colleagues speaking one day about how improvement science was a linear, positivist, White man's way of thinking and I took great offense because, as a Black woman, I have embraced this methodology wholeheartedly. As a Black woman who lives in the various intersections of race, gender, and class, I understand the complexities of systems. I understand some things are outside of what I can control. But, more so, I understand I come from a people who have always managed to operate terrain not built for them. We have long understood, as Rev. Dr. King preached in May of 1956 at the Cathedral of St. John the Divine in New York City, "Change does not roll in on the wheels of inevitability, but comes through continuous struggle." We have to be part of the struggle; we have to be catalysts for change.

We, Black people in general, and Black women specifically, have always tried to push to make systemic changes while identifying immediate changes we can make to improve right now. It is pushing for criminal justice reform and bias training for police while also teaching your son to keep his hands out of his pockets, not make any sudden moves, and be hyper-respectful when dealing with law enforcement. It is questioning the validity of admissions tests and advocating for their abolishment while also prepping your child for the test. It is fighting for a living wage while working multiple jobs. Historically, and contemporarily, we have had to do both.

Pushing the primary driver forward with our eye on the ultimate aim is what has been embedded in me. We've always had a view toward the long game. When King talked about the mountaintop, he understood it was off in the distance. When Ella Baker said, "We who believe in freedom cannot rest until it comes," she understood that it was not one bullet, one protest, one piece of legislation that was going to make it all better. But the fight for justice and equality is iterative and continuous. But iterative does not mean slow or stalling; it means constantly reviewing the strategy to get to the goal faster. The strategy may change as we try things and they don't work; we tweak it, and we move forward.

Deming is considered the father of quality improvement. Bryk and fellow associates were in the Carnegie Foundation and are key architects of the way we are understanding the applicability of improving science in education. However, my embrace of improvement science happened because it aligned with the relentless persistence that has always yearned in my soul and been exemplified by those I most admire. I am in education and I use research, not for fame or notoriety, but to truly understand or to truly aid me in assisting those in the margins. I would never tell teachers and parents and administrators that they should quail in their fight for systemic change—better policy, better funding, better facilities. While that fight rages on, it is important for us to find high leverage changes, immediate improvements we can make now that will benefit our children. So, while the stereotype is you don't see a great deal of Black women statisticians, we've always paid attention to variation. We've had to measure variation in temperament of men to ensure our safety; we've watched fluctuation in the price of eggs and we have balanced the budget—to us, this is not new.

To some, improvement science may look like it's a White man's way of thinking. But I'm writing about it as a Black girl. A southern Black girl raised by a southern Black woman with a heart for children, who believes that this is a tool that could aid me in my quest to decrease disparities in access to opportunities for children in the margins. So, you say, "why is this Black woman writing about improving science?" There you have it. That's why I embrace the task of writing a primer so that someone intimidated by *The Improvement Guide* or someone still unclear on what to do while reading *Learning to Improve* has somewhere to start. This primer is somewhere to get the basics, the building blocks. I hope you found that I introduced it in a way that made it accessible, because if you can access it, you can use it. If you can use it, you can make real change for our children. I appreciate your reading it but, even more so, I appreciate your using disciplined inquiries to guide your improvements, and—I challenge you to use it with an unquenchable thirst for justice.

Walker, A. (1983). *In search of our mothers' gardens: Womanist prose*. San Diego, CA: Harcourt Inc.

Glossary

- **Aim**—An aim statement is a succinct description of the desired outcomes that answers the questions: What? For whom? By when? And by how much?

- **Before-and-After/Pre-test-Post-test design**—The before-and-after or pre-test-post-test design is one of multiple research designs that can be employed within a PDSA cycle. It establishes a baseline (pretest), employs a change, and then compares the outcomes after the change with the baseline.

- **Change**—Change is the act of making or becoming different. All improvement requires change; all change does not result in improvement.

- **Change concept**—Change concepts are categories that capture multiple change ideas and show underlying approaches to systematic change.

- **Change idea**—A change idea is an idea about how to generate change in your current system.

- **Charter**—A charter is a guiding document that outlines the goals, theory, measurement, and methods of an improvement initiative.

- **Common cause**—A common cause leads to less than desirable but stable outcomes. Common causes are flaws within the system. Deming suggests 94% of possibilities for improvement are due to common causes or systematic flaws.

- **Complexity**—Complexity is used to describe and understand systems. A systems complexity is a result of its multiplicity (number of parts), diversity or heterogeneity of those parts, and the degree of their interdependence.

- **Constructivism**—Constructivism, often associated with qualitative research, is a research paradigm that asserts truth is constructed, and the truth varies depending on perspective.

- **Critical, participatory, advocacy, and emancipatory research**—Critical, participatory, advocacy, and emancipatory research paradigms are concerned with social change. The objective of this research is to elevate the voice of marginalized, and to do research *with* and not *on* marginalized populations.

- **Deductive reasoning**—Deductive reasoning begins with theory and moves from theory, to data, to confirmation or revision of the theory.

- **Deficit ideology**—Deficit ideology, also known as deficit perspective and deficit cognitive frame, is a worldview that rationalizes and justifies inequitable outcomes as the result of deficiencies within individuals or their communities instead of broader systems. It is a form of "blaming the victim" that is rooted in hegemonic/dominant beliefs about superiority and inferiority. While deficit ideology was once rooted in eugenics and belief in genetic inferiority, it has morphed to beliefs in cultural inferiority. Deficit ideology would espouse a statement such as: poor people are poor because they are lazy.

- **Design team**—Improvement science is not a personal project; it is collaborative in nature. To design impactful changes, practitioners must rely on the expertise of a wide array of stakeholders. A design team is a team of stakeholders who possess the knowledge to understand (define) problems and design (develop) solutions within an organization.

- **Design thinking**—Design thinking is one of many methods used to generate ideas for change and improvement. Design thinking can be viewed as three distinct phases: inspiration, ideation, and implementation.

- **Design-based implementation research (DBIR)**—DBIR is an improvement methodology that seeks to address persistent problems of practice by bridging the divide between scholars and practitioners to decrease the distance between innovation and implementation. It is guided by four principles and has no prescribed methodology. Improvement science can be the methodological approach employed in DBIR.

- **Diversity Scorecard**—A Diversity Scorecard is a tool to help educators, mainly in higher education, view inequities within their organizations. Bensimon (2004) describes the tool as having three purposes—to prompt awareness, to interpret, and to support action to resolve inequities in a collegiate setting.

- **Driver diagram**—A driver diagram is a tool that illustrates the theory of improvement (also known as a theory of practice improvement) that contains the desired outcomes, key parts of the system that influence the outcome, and possible changes that will yield desirable results.

- **Drivers**—Drivers are elements within a system that influence the desired outcome, or aim.

- **Emergence**—Emergence is a concept that suggests the system is more than the sum of the separate parts within the system.

- **Empathy interviews**—Empathy interviews are a qualitative data collection technique that helps practitioners understand the perspectives of different stakeholders. They can be used during problem definition, as a part of seeing the system, or as a method to document implementation within the PDSA cycle. While advanced by design schools, empathy interviews are similar to qualitative interviewing techniques especially ethnographic and phenomenological approaches to research.

- **Equity audit**—Equity audits are guides to examining data to determine where inequities may persist. Proportional representation is often a barometer for determining the extent of disproportionality or inequity in a particular domain.

- **External validity**—External validity is often referred to as generalizability. External validity answers the question: Are the study's findings true (accurate) for those outside of the study?

- **Factorial design**—A factorial design is one of multiple research designs that can be employed during PDSA cycles. A factorial design is appropriate when more than one change is being assessed at a time. It helps practitioners estimate individual effects of each change as well as interaction effects.

- **Fishbone/Ishikawa diagram**—The fishbone diagram is a tool for delineating root causes of a particular problem of practice.

- **Five Whys technique**—The Five Whys technique is a root cause analysis process that helps practitioners get to the source of a problem by asking why—five times.

- **Fundamental change**—Fundamental change is change that leads the system to a new (hopefully more desirable) level of performance.

- **Generalizability**—Generalizability asks to what extent a study's findings generalize to other contexts. It is also known as external validity.

- **Implementation science**—Implementation science is an improvement methodology that seeks to understand variance in program outcomes due to implementation.

- **Implementation team**—An implementation team is a team of stakeholders within an organization, tasked with implementing a change (intervention, new process, new technology) as a part of the improvement science process.

- **Improvement science**—Improvement science is a methodological framework that is undergirded by foundational principles guiding scholar-practitioners to define problems, understand how the system produces the problems, identify changes to rectify the problems, test the efficacy of those changes, and spread the changes (if the change is indeed an improvement).

- **Inclusive Excellence Scorecard**—An Inclusive Excellence Scorecard is a tool to help educators, primarily in higher education, view inequities within their organizations. The IE Scorecard has four areas for assessment: access and equity, campus climate, diversity in formal and informal curricula, and learning and development.

- **Inductive reasoning**—Inductive reasoning begins with data or observations, and moves from data, to patterns, to theory.

- **Internal validity**—Interval validity deals with the question: *Are the findings true (or accurate) for the participants in the study?* In quantitative research, where there is a treatment administered or a particular covariate in question, validity is determined when no other factor can be argued to influence the outcome besides the variable in question.

- **Intervention**—Intervention is often synonymous with change; it is how you plan to intercede in the system to create improvement.

- **Iterative cycles**—Iterative cycles are one of the hallmarks of improvement science process. They illustrate the continuousness of continuous improvement, as each cycle is informed by the previous cycle.

- **Lean Six Sigma**—Lean Six Sigma is an integration of two improvement methodologies, Lean, which focuses on a reduction of waste, and Six Sigma, which focuses on a reduction in process variation.

- **Lesson study**—Lesson study is an improvement methodology designed to improve instruction. The collaborative method, designed for teachers, consists of a four-step cycle that begins with studying curricula and formulating goals, developing a plan (lesson) that will achieve the goals, studying the lesson (as implemented in a real classroom), and then reflecting on the process. Educators can revise and reteach the lesson as needed.

- **Logical negative thinking**—Logical negative thinking is critical in nature; it focuses on potential barriers and setbacks to implementing a new change.

- **Logical positive thinking**—Logical positive thinking is optimistic in nature, and focuses on how to get new ideas to work.

- **Measurement for accountability**—Measurement for accountability is usually a lagging indicator, collected at the end of some cycle (academic year, term, semester). Measurement for accountability is tied to rewards and sanctions.

- **Measurement for improvement**—Measurement for improvement or practical measurement is data collected to inform improvement efforts. They operationalize the theory of improvement. Practical measures are collected frequently, embedded in day-to-day tasks, and are written in a language for various stakeholders to understand. Four practical measures are used in improvement science: outcome measures, driver measures, balancing measures, and process measures.

- **Measurement for research**—Measurement for research consists of instruments created to measure latent constructs to be used in the testing and modeling of theory. Research instruments are often characterized as being long batteries of items, with multiple items trying to assess the same latent underlying trait.

- **Model for Improvement**—The Model for Improvement (MFI) is advanced in the text, *The Improvement Guide*. The MFI is the interplay of the three essential improvement science questions (What am I trying to accomplish? How will I know if a change is an improvement? What change might I introduce and why?) and the PDSA methodology.

- **Network improvement community**—An NIC community is an execution network (as opposed to a sharing network), designed to address a particular aim. The networks collaboratively address problems of practice in an effort to accelerate improvement.

- **Network initiation team**—A network initiation team is a group committed to establishing a network improvement community. The team does some of the initial work of the NIC such as defining the problem, studying the system, and outlining the theory of improvement. They may also create guiding documents such as a network charter that outlines requirements for membership.

- **Observational design**—An observational design is one of multiple research designs that can be employed within the PDSA cycle. In this design, you compare two groups after employing a change or intervention with one group, to see how they differ. It is similar to a quasi-experiment.

- **Opportunity gaps**—Opportunity gaps are not synonymous with achievement gaps. Gaps in achievement are often symptoms of gaps in opportunity. The phrase opportunity gap is used to describe differential access to resources and educational opportunities experienced by different groups of students.

- **Outcome measures**—Outcome measures measure outcomes. They are lagging measures that answer the question: *Did it work?*

- **Outcome variation**—Outcome variation is instability in desired outcomes.

- **Pareto chart**—A pareto chart is useful when examining sources or causes for variation (particularly errors). It is a bar chart with a line graph superimposed. The bar represents counts of particular causes or errors, and the line graph illustrates the cumulative percentage of the whole each bar represents. The Pareto Principle says 80% of variation is due to 20% of the causes; a Pareto chart helps you determine if this is the case, and can help you prioritize what issues to address first.

- **Participant observer**—In ethnographic or observational research, a participant observer is one who has dual roles; they are involved with the phenomenon under investigation as well as being an investigator. They have to pay close attention to what is happening to accurately capture events and processes, and must try, to the extent possible, to document their role and influence on what transpires. They use fieldnotes (journals, maps, video diaries, etc.) to try to accurately capture with the least amount of bias.

- **PDCA/FOCUS PDCA**—The PDCA is a continuous improvement cycle—Plan-Do-Check and Act that originates in Japan. The distinction between the PDSA and the PDCA cycle is that PDCAs look more narrowly at faults within system processes, whereas the PDSA had a broader application (processes, products, programs, etc.). The FOCUS PDCA is similar to the *Model for Improvement*, as it has five steps preceding the PDCA methodology, as the three essential questions lead into the PDSA cycle.

- **PDSA cycle**—The Plan-Do-Study-Act cycle is the signature improvement science methodology. It combines deductive and inductive forms of inquiry in iterative cycles to improve problems of practice. It has four distinct phases, from which its name is derived, planning, doing, studying, and acting.

- **Positivism/post-positivism**—Positivism is an approach to research (research paradigm) that asserts a truth does exist. Positivism is predecessor of post-positivism, which also believes truth exists, but in post-positivism, researchers can never be certain that they have reached the truth.

- **Practical measurement**—Practical measurement or *measurement for improvement* is data collected to inform improvement efforts. They operationalize the theory of improvement. Practical measures are collected frequently, embedded in day-to-day tasks, and are written in a language for various stakeholders to understand. Four practical measures are used in improvement science: outcome measures, driver measures, balancing measures, and process measures.

- **Pragmatism**—Pragmatism is a research paradigm concerned with how research and its findings can be applied to improve practical functions. Essentially, pragmatists seek to answer the question: What works?

- **Process map**—A process map is a flowchart that illustrates the processes (and in some cases responsible parties) within a complex system.

- **Process measures**—Process measures are often measures of fidelity, ensuring process variation is under control. They answer the question: *How is it working?*

- **Process variation**—Process variation deals with change or fluidity in an organizational process or in the implementation of some intervention. Sometimes the goal of an improvement is to minimize process variation.

- **Psychologism**—Psychologism is the blending of psychology and logic.

- **Qualitative research**—Qualitative research is an approach to research designed to generate theory by exploring phenomenon in detail and providing thick, rich descriptions. The goal is depth not breadth.

- **Quantitative research**—Quantitative research generally tests theories. Quantitative research seeks to uncover general truths that can explain phenomena in most circumstances. There is a premium on parsimony, explaining a phenomenon with as few variables as possible. The goal of quantitative research, in most cases, is to be generalizable.

- **Reactive change**—Reactive change is change that is necessary to maintain the system's current level of performance.

- **Root cause analysis (RCA)**—Root cause analysis is a process for determining the underlying source for a problem. Root cause analysis is necessary when practitioners believe undesired outcomes are merely a symptom of a fundamental problem. There are many different approaches to root cause analysis.

- **Run chart**—A run chart is a line graph where researchers plot data on outcomes or processes over time (daily, weekly, etc.). A run chart also illustrates a median line for reference to determine when there are runs, shifts, and trends.

- **Run**—A run is a series of points on a run chart clustered on one side of the median.

- **Scholar practitioner**—A scholar practitioner is a practitioner who guides their practice with scholarship and disciplined inquiry. A scholar practitioner is a reflective practitioner always seeking to improve their organization and their individual practice.

- **Shift**—A shift is when there are six or more consecutive points on the same side of the median.

- **Six Sigma**—Six Sigma is an improvement methodology that seeks to reduce process variation that leads to negative outcomes.

- **Small-scale tests**—Small-scale tests are another hallmark of improvement science. Embedded in this strategy is the desire to ensure that a change/intervention is efficacious before implementing on a large scale. Furthermore, with each test, practitioners learn more about the change and the process of implementation—and that information can inform efforts to spread.

- **Solutionitis**—Solutionitis is the propensity of educators to jump to solutions before fully defining (understanding) the problem.

- **Special cause**—A special cause is change in variation due to a specific localized cause.

- **System**—A system is an entity (organization) made of interconnected parts bound by a common purpose.

- **System of profound knowledge**—To make improvement in an organization, W. E. Deming said individuals need two types of knowledge: subject matter knowledge and profound knowledge. The system of profound knowledge, wedded throughout the principles of improvement, includes four facets: appreciation for systems, knowledge of variation, a theory of knowledge, and psychology (or knowledge about people).

- **Systems diagram**—A systems diagram is a visual schematic to help illustrate circles of influence within systems, scaffolding systems thinkers away from linear understandings of cause and effect.

- **Systems map**—A system map illustrates the components and boundaries of a system.

- **Systems thinking**—Systems thinking is an approach to viewing problems as the result of systems and helps to illuminate the variety of systems at play in complex situations.

- **Theory of action**—A theory of action is a localized theory that explains how a change should happen in a particular context.

- **Theory of change**—A theory of change is a localized theory that explains why a change should happen in a particular context.

- **Theory of improvement**—A theory of improvement is a localized theory that explains the why and how of a particular intervention, considering the system that is producing the problem, the knowledge of those who will implement the intervention, and theories (with a capital T) and empirical research on the problem.

- **Theory of knowledge**—A theory of knowledge outlines the theories and subject matter knowledge necessary to improve in a particular context.

- **Time series design**—A time series design in one of multiple research designs that can be employed within a PDSA framework. Similar to single-subject research, it follows the data on outcomes or processes over time. It examines the variation during the introduction of an intervention and the removal of that intervention.

- **Trend**—A trend is five or more points on a run chart moving in the same direction.

- **True experiment**—A true experiment is a study that compares the outcomes of two groups: a treatment group and a control group. These two groups are assigned using random assignment, meaning everyone in the sample has an equal chance of being assigned to either group. The treatment group experiences some treatment or intervention where the control group does not. The outcomes of the two groups are compared. True experiments, or randomized controlled trials, are considered the goal standard in research. Quasi-experiments are a similar research design, but lack the random assignment.

- **User-centered**—To be user-centered, or user-centric, is to seek to understand problems of practice and solutions from the perspectives of those closest to the problem.

- **Validity**—Validity means accuracy. Conceptually, it deals with the question of whether findings from a particular study can be trusted. Quantitative research deals with two types of validity: internal validity and external validity. Qualitative research uses different criteria for evaluation and is assessed by its descriptive validity, interpretive validity, and trustworthiness.

INDEX